Mission Viejo Library
25209 Marguerite Parkway
Mission Viejo, CA 92691

JUN 0 7 1999

SO-BIR-263

Crazy Horse

Also by Larry McMurtry
in Large Print:

Anything for Billy
Buffalo Girls
Comanche Moon
Dead Man's Walk
The Evening Star
Some Can Whistle
Streets of Laredo
Terms of Endearment

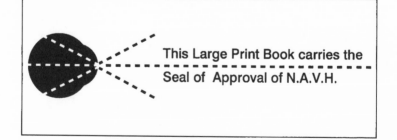

This Large Print Book carries the
Seal of Approval of N.A.V.H.

LARRY McMURTRY

Crazy Horse

Thorndike Press • Thorndike, Maine

Copyright © Larry McMurtry, 1999

All rights reserved.

Published in 1999 by arrangement with Viking Penguin, a division of Penguin Putnam Inc.

Thorndike Large Print ® Basic Series.

The tree indicium is a trademark of Thorndike Press.

The text of this Large Print edition is unabridged.
Other aspects of the book may vary from the original edition.

Set in 16 pt. Plantin.

Printed in the United States on permanent paper.

Library of Congress Cataloging in Publication Data

McMurtry, Larry.
 Crazy Horse / Larry McMurtry. — Large print ed.
  p. cm.
 ISBN 0-7862-1901-7 (lg. print : hc : alk. paper)
 1. Crazy Horse, ca. 1842–1877. 2. Oglala Indians —
Kings and rulers — Biography. I. Title.
 [E99.O3C7246 1999b]
 978′.0049752′0092—dc21   99-18817

For Leslie Marmon Silko

1

Crazy Horse, a Sioux warrior dead more than one hundred and twenty years, buried no one knows where, is rising again over Pa Sapa, the Black Hills of South Dakota, holy to the Sioux. Today, as in life, his horse is with him. Fifty years of effort on the part of the sculptor Korczak Ziolkowski and his wife and children have just begun to nudge the man and his horse out of what was once Thunderhead Mountain. In the half-century that the Ziolkowski family has worked, millions of tons of rock have been moved, as they attempt to create what will be the world's largest sculpture; but the man that is emerging from stone and dirt is as yet only a suggestion, a shape, which those who journey to Custer, South Dakota, to see must complete in their own imaginations.

It is a nice irony that the little town Crazy Horse has come to brood over is named for his old adversary George Armstrong Custer — Long Hair, whose hair, however, had been cut short on the day of

7

his last battle, so that it is not certain that the Sioux or Cheyenne who killed him really recognized him until after he was dead. Crazy Horse had one good look at Custer, in a skirmish on the Yellowstone River in 1873, but Custer probably never saw Crazy Horse clearly enough to have identified him, either on the Yellowstone or at the Little Bighorn, three years later. The thousands who come to the Crazy Horse Monument each year see him as yet only vaguely; but that, too, will change. One day his arm will stretch out almost the length of a football field; statistics will accumulate around his mountain just as legends, rumors, true tales and tall tales, accumulated around the living man.

What should be stressed at the outset is that Crazy Horse was loved and valued by his people as much for his charity as for his courage. Ian Frazier, in his fine book *Great Plains*, reports correctly that the Crazy Horse Monument is one of the few places on the Great Plains where one will see a lot of Indians smiling. The knowledge of his charity is still a balm to his people, the Sioux people, most of whom are poor and all of whom are oppressed. Peter Matthiessen was right to call his bitterly trenchant report on the troubles the Pine

Ridge Sioux had with the U.S. government in the 1970s *In the Spirit of Crazy Horse*, because the spirit of Crazy Horse was a spirit unbroken, though it was certainly raked raw by the difficulties of his last few months.

George E. Hyde, the great (if cranky) historian of the Oglala and the Brulé Sioux, a man not easily swept off his feet by even the most potent myth, confessed his puzzlement with the Crazy Horse legend in words that are neither unfair nor inaccurate: "They depict Crazy Horse as a kind of being never seen on earth: a genius at war yet a lover of peace; a statesman who apparently never thought of the interest of any human being outside his own camp; a dreamer, a mystic, and a kind of Sioux Christ, who was betrayed in the end by his own disciples — Little Big Man, Touch-the-Clouds and the rest. One is inclined to ask, what is it all about?"

A Sioux Christ? That touches on his charity and on his betrayal, but he was a determined warrior too, one of the great Resisters, men who do not compromise, do not negotiate, do not administer, who exist in a realm beyond the give-and-take of conventional politics and who stumble and are defeated only when hard circumstances force them to live in that realm.

I saw the Crazy Horse Monument one day while traveling north to visit the grave of that sad, boastful woman Martha Jane Canary (Calamity Jane), who lies in the Deadwood cemetery next to James Butler Hickok (Wild Bill), a proximity he could not protest, since Calamity outlived him by a quarter of a century. I was easing through the Black Hills buffalo herd — many of the buffalo stood in the road, dull and incurious, as indifferent to the traffic as they had been to the buffalo hunters who slaughtered some fifty million of them in a short space of time in the last century — when I slowly became aware of something: something large. I looked up and saw the Crazy Horse mountain, just to the northeast. Great hundred-yard swirls of white paint streaked the mountain, representing his hair; below him more swirls of the same white paint formed a Picassoesque horse head.

Like most travelers who come unexpectedly onto the monument, I was stunned, too stunned even to go up to the gift shop. I stopped the car, sat on the hood, and looked, as buffalo ambled by. What loomed above me, framed by the blue Dakota sky, was an American Sphinx. He was there, but as a force, an indefiniteness, a form made more powerful by his very abstractness.

I suppose, someday, the Ziolkowski family will finish this statue. It may take another generation or two, and when it's finished, if I'm alive, I'd like to see it. But I'm glad that I saw the mountain in the years when Crazy Horse was still only a form and a mystery. Now that I've read what there is to read about him, I think this indefiniteness was also an aspect of the man. His own people experienced him as a mystery while he was alive: they called him Our Strange Man. In his life he would have three names: Curly, His Horses Looking, Crazy Horse (Ta-Shunka-Witco). We know him as Crazy Horse, but in life few knew him well; in truth it is only in a certain limited way that we who are living now can know him at all. George Hyde, who resisted his legend, knew that in spite of what he himself wrote, time had already separated the myth from the man, obliterating fact. Fair or not, that is the way with heroes: Geronimo, Crazy Horse, Sitting Bull, Billy the Kid, Custer. For all such men, fact withers in the heat of myth. George Hyde felt the frustrations all historians feel when they find a legend blocking

11

their route to what had once only been a man.

Crazy Horse's legend grew *in the main* from a broken people's need to remember and believe in unbroken heroes, those who remained true to the precepts of their fathers and to the ways of the culture and the traditions which bred them.

Certainly the whites who fought Crazy Horse helped build his legend, too. Agent Jesse Lee, who brought Crazy Horse back from the Spotted Tail agency to Fort Robinson, only to see him killed before he could be given the hearing that had been promised him, confessed that he was tortured by his involvement in such a dark deed. Even the stern General Crook, who, had he caught him alive, would have sent Crazy Horse off to a prison in the Dry Tortugas — all on the basis of a lie — later expressed regret that he had failed to sit in council with him on the last occasion that presented itself. "I ought to have gone to that council," Crook said. "I never start any place but that I get there."

This short book is an attempt to look back across more than one hundred and twenty years at the life and death of the Sioux warrior Crazy Horse, the man who is coming out of a mountain in the Black

Hills, the American Sphinx, the loner who has inspired the largest sculpture on planet Earth. It will be an attempt to answer George Hyde's pointed question: What was it all about?

2

It is as well to say firmly at the outset that any study of Crazy Horse will be, of necessity, an exercise in assumption, conjecture, and surmise. We have more verifiable facts about another young warrior, Alexander, called the Great, who lived more than two thousand years earlier than Crazy Horse and whose career is also richly encrusted with legend, than we do about the strange man of the Oglalas (to adopt Mari Sandoz's phrase). Crazy Horse lived about three and a half decades as a member of a hunting-raiding-gathering tribe that was not at all date obsessed. The dates and places where the historian can firmly place him are white dates: mainly the dates of a few battles he is known to have taken part in. For most of his life he not only avoided white people, he avoided people, spending many days alone on the prairies, dreaming, drifting, hunting. According to Short Buffalo, a fellow Sioux who knew him well, he was "not very tall and not very short, neither broad nor thin. His hair was very light . . . Crazy Horse had a very light complexion, much lighter than other Indians. His face was not broad, and he had a high, sharp nose. He had black eyes that hardly ever looked straight at a man, but they didn't miss much that was going on, all the same. . . ."

There was something of the hermit, the eremite, in him; he was known to walk through his own camp without appearing to notice anybody. When, late in his life, his family began to worry about his tendency to wander off alone in dangerous country, he told them not to worry, there were plenty of caves and holes he could live in; and had it not been for his sense of responsibility to the people of his village — who knew that he would do his best to feed them — he might well have slipped away and lived in those caves and holes.

He came into Fort Robinson, in northwestern Nebraska, with the nine hundred people who, in desperation, had chosen to follow him, only *four months* before he was killed, and those four months were the only period in his life when he was in contact with the record-keeping, letter-writing whites; and even then, he camped six miles from the fort, rather than the prescribed three, and saw whites only when he could not avoid them. For almost the whole of his life he did avoid all parleys, councils, treaty sessions, and any meeting of an administrative or political nature, not merely with whites but with his own people as well.

Although he was given the great honor of being a Shirt-wearer, a position whose responsibilities he fulfilled as best he could by providing for the weak and helpless ones of the tribe, he was never a talker; for most of his life we know nothing at all of what he said or thought. He was a loner — now, in many respects, he is a blank. Professional writers and amateur historians, professional historians and amateur writers, have all written about him extensively and have not scrupled to put words in his mouth and even to report his dreams — or, at least, one dream that was of great significance in shaping the way he lived his life.

The basis for most of these conversations, reports, speculations are two sets of interviews with elderly Sioux, both sets to be found in the archives of the Nebraska State Historical Association. The first set was done by Judge Eli Ricker in 1906–07; the second, by the journalist Elinor Hinman and the Nebraska writer Mari Sandoz in 1930–31. Judge Ricker interviewed about fifty people, of whom only ten were Indian. The core of the Hinman-Sandoz interviews is the one with He Dog (brother of Short Buffalo), a life-long friend of Crazy Horse. He Dog was in his nineties when the interviews were conducted; he outlived his friend Crazy Horse by fifty-nine years (Libbie Custer outlived her George by fifty-seven). He Dog may indeed have had a remarkable memory, but to ask him to look back over almost ninety years to the boyhood of his friend was asking a lot — and, anyway, the interviewers devoted most of their questions to the crucial last fifteen months of Crazy Horse's life, when the famous battles were fought. Except for one or two incidents, the other thirty-five years of his life are barely touched on; and the interview, all told, is only about fifteen pages long, questions included. Mari Sandoz then wrote a biography which is 428 pages long, many of them purely speculative. Stephen Ambrose, a professional historian, writing in the mid-seventies, devotes about half of a 538-page book to Crazy Horse, and, like Sandoz, doesn't seem to mind putting words in the mouth of this man of few words.

If the word "record" is to mean any-thing, one would have to say that for much of Crazy Horse's life there is no record. He lived the life of a Sioux warrior, raiding and hunting on the central plains. Then, as white pressure on the Plains Indians began to intensify, Crazy Horse emerged as a determined resister whose courage and leadership was a factor in a few battles.

From 1875 on, the record grows steadily more dense, reaching maximum density only on the last day of his life. More has been written about his death — far more — than about the other three and a half decades of his life put together. This is perhaps only natural: there were many witnesses to his fatal stabbing, whereas most of his life went unwitnessed by anyone who would have had any reason to take notes.

The accounts of his death are so many and so varied that one could make a kind of Gospels of Crazy Horse, or, at least, an American *Rashomon*.

There is also — rarely mentioned but critical — the huge problem of translation. The old men who were looking back across the years and yielding up their memories of Crazy Horse did so in the Sioux language, a language seldom easily or accurately brought into English. Twice in his life, once when he was a young man and

19

once near the end, Crazy Horse experienced the destructiveness that could result from sloppy, inaccurate, or biased interpretation. The slippage between the two languages as the result of ill-intended or merely vague translation was a source of huge frustration to the Indians who made themselves available at the treaty councils — Red Cloud and Spotted Tail in particular — and then found out that what they thought they had heard the whites promise was not in fact what they were getting. How much harder is it, then, for us who really don't know his words, to trust that we know what this private man — who rarely spoke, even in the councils of his own people — felt or thought?

All this is not to say that we know nothing of Crazy Horse. He was a man, not a myth, and we do know certain things about him. We know enough from the testimony of his close associates to have some idea of the main events of his life, particularly his losses: of his brother Little Hawk, of his daughter They-Are-Afraid-of-Her, of his friends Hump and Lone Bear, and of Black Buffalo Woman, the love of his life, who married another man. We also know something of his behavior in two or three crucial battles.

Still, I am not writing this book because I think I know what Crazy Horse did — much less what he thought — on more than a few occasions in his life; I'm writing it because I have some notions about what he meant to his people in his lifetime, and also what he has come to mean to generations of Sioux in our century and even our time.

Ian Frazier, in discussing what he left *out* of his meditation on Crazy Horse, admits that he omitted a story about Crazy Horse kneeling to Crook the first time the two men met. He left it out, he says, because (a) he didn't completely believe it and (b) he didn't like it. Any biographer of Crazy Horse who has done due diligence with the record will at times be likely to apply that standard in judging this report or that.

I would also like to suggest that the traditions of genre exert their force here and there in the historical record. The genre I have in mind is the battle report, which falls back, if unconsciously, on Homer. When Stephen Ambrose says that forty thousand arrows were shot during the twenty or thirty minutes that it took the Sioux and Cheyenne to kill all the soldiers in the Fetterman massacre, I feel that what I'm getting is a trope, not a fact. Who would have been counting arrows on that cold day in Wyoming in 1866?

In the Crazy Horse literature, as well as the literature of the Plains Indians in general, the historians often chide the writers — Mari Sandoz, Evan S. Connell Jr., John G. Neihardt — for producing good writing but bad history; the writers seldom bother to chide back. The literature of Crazy Horse is about evenly divided between that produced by "writers" and that produced by "historians." Neither, so far, have convinced many readers — and certainly not this reader — that they have an accurate grip on the deeds, much less on the soul, of the Sioux warrior we call Crazy Horse.

3

The Sioux peoples in the time of Crazy Horse were spread across the northern and central plains in many loosely related tribes of bands, each governed, for the most part, not by one leader but by councils composed of tribal elders, men of skill, experience, and wisdom.

I am going to do my best, in this narrative, to avoid blanketing my pages under a blizzard of nomenclature in an attempt to precisely delineate the many bands, groups, villages that then flowed back and forth across the Great Plains. The Sioux were a mobile people who saw little advantage in rigidly fixed arrangements. Crazy Horse was an Oglala who spent a lot of time with the Brulés (his mother's people), some time with the Cheyennes, and, later in his life, at least a little time with the Hunkpapas. One of the glories of being a Plains Indian in his time was that one didn't have to stay put. An Oglala might want to move in with the Minniconjou band for a while, and was free to do so.

The people were of necessity on the move anyway — the necessity being the dictates of the hunt. Crazy Horse as a teenager was on more than one occasion lectured for foolishly endangering himself by going off alone; but, like many teenagers, he continued to go where he pleased, and he frequently endangered himself.

He was born around 1840, by the Belle Fourche River, near Bear Butte, in what is now South Dakota. Chips, or Encouraging Bear, a Sioux medicine man, thought he had been born in the year when the Sioux had captured many horses from the Shoshones; this big raid occurred in 1841. Bear Butte was a favorite gathering place for several bands of the Sioux.

One aspect of Sioux nomenclature that is apt to confuse the reader (it is particularly confusing in Mari Sandoz's biography) is that a warrior didn't ordinarily acquire his permanent name until he had grown up and done something to earn it. Crazy Horse's father was also called Crazy Horse; the father didn't transfer this name to his son until he had proven himself valorous in battle, after which the father was known as Worm. So it was, too, with Sitting Bull, the Hunkpapa, whose childhood nickname was Slow and whose formal name was Jumping Badger; once the boy had counted coup, his father allowed him to become Sitting Bull.

He Dog, Short Buffalo, and several others mentioned that Crazy Horse was unusually light-complexioned, so much so that he was sometimes referred to as the Light-Skinned Boy. The same friends, and several whites as well, mentioned that he was not tall, and that he had sharp features. From an early age he was said to have a touch with horses, good at stealing them from other tribes and good, also, at capturing and breaking wild horses. Thanks to this skill he was for a time given the name His Horses Looking, but that name never caught on.

Worm, his father, was not a warrior. He was a healer, a shaman, a holy man, and an accomplished interpreter of dreams. Little is known about Crazy Horse's mother — she was thought to be the sister of Spotted Tail, the Brulé leader who sat in many councils and was one of the first Sioux to conclude that it was futile to fight the whites. It was to Spotted Tail's agency that Crazy Horse fled just before he was killed; but Spotted Tail, wanting no trouble, was stern with his nephew and was part of the escort that took him back to Fort Robinson.

It is worth noting that Crazy Horse was not born into one of the great families of the Sioux, families that had become great through much raiding and the capture of many horses. Worm's lodge was humble. Stephen Ambrose argues correctly that the Sioux were a tolerant, noncompulsive people. Individuals were allowed to follow their own bent; that different people had differing abilities was recognized and accepted. Worm's counsel was valued — he did not have to be a warrior to earn the tribe's respect.

Crazy Horse, from the first, was indifferent to tribal norms. He had no interest, early or late, in the annual sundance rite, and didn't bother with any of the ordeals of purification that many young Sioux men underwent, rituals that have been well recorded by George Catlin and others. Crazy Horse took his manhood as a given, and proved it in battle from an early age. His people may have thought him strange, but nonetheless he was let alone, allowed to walk in his own way.

His prominence today, as a symbol of Sioux resistance, owes much to his character, of course, but it also is in part a matter of historical timing. He fought his best in the last great battles — the Rosebud and the Little Bighorn — and then died young, in the last moments when the Sioux could think of themselves as free. By an accident of fate, the man and the way of life died together: little wonder that he came to be a symbol of Sioux freedom, Sioux courage, and Sioux dignity.

Though Crazy Horse was able to live many months and sometimes even years in the traditional Sioux way, raiding and hunting in turn, the way of life to which he had been born was dying even while he was a boy. By the time of his birth the whites were already moving in considerable numbers along the Holy Road (what we call the Oregon Trail); at first the pressure of white intrusion may have been subtle and slight, but it was present, and would be present throughout his entire life. The buffalo were there in their millions when he was born but were mostly gone by the time he died. Crazy Horse would have been a boy of five or six when Francis Parkman camped in a Sioux village whose leader was Old Smoke; it's possible that young Curly — Crazy Horse's nickname while a boy — was even living in the village when Parkman passed through. We don't know that, but we do know that Francis Parkman was well aware that the way of life he was witnessing that summer — vividly described in *The Oregon Trail* — was a way of life that would soon be changing; indeed, would soon end.

As a lad Curly probably had no inkling of this, nor did most of his people, although the presence of whites in increasing numbers along the Holy Road was already an irritant. With such an abundance of game both north and south of the Platte River, it may be thought that tribal life could have gone on with little change. But the lives of hunting people are never that secure. There was, to be sure, a lot of game; but it didn't meekly present itself to those who hunted it. The game still had to be found and killed — then as now, animals were quick to shift away from places where they were heavily hunted. From the standpoint of the Sioux, Cheyenne, and Pawnee hunters who lived by what they killed, the white invasion was almost immediately destructive.

Very early too, even from the time of the first fur traders, an unfortunate symbiosis began to develop between tribes and traders. The whites had goods that the Indians wanted — goods on which they soon became dependent. Lord Raglan, the sharp-spoken English anthropologist and myth theorist, has commented acutely on the fragility of hunting cultures in a book called *How Came Civilization?* He points out that peoples who had been adept for generations at making bone fishhooks lose this skill very quickly once they are supplied with metal fishhooks. The Plains Indians soon came to like needles and other small tools that could be had in quantity from traders who frequented the forts and gathering places along the Holy Road.

Sitting Bull, the very tough-minded Hunkpapa, perhaps had the clearest vision of the ultimate destructiveness of trade with the white man; he saw very early that it would soon destroy Sioux independence, and he was right. He always counseled his people to have nothing to do with the whites and to stay as far away from them as possible. But, unfortunately, the westward course of empire (a fine phrase that covered over much brutality) left the Sioux little choice. In time, and not much time, the whites were everywhere.

As soon as the first forts were established along the Holy Road, and certainly after the great Laramie council of 1851, there were what came to be called ration Indians, of coffee coolers, those who lived by the forts and let go the strenuous, uncertain life of the hunt; in giving up the life of the warrior Sioux, they soon forfeited much of the respect of those tribesmen who still hunted and fought.

By 1850 all the Plains Indians had to reckon with the fact that though the whites were going through, they weren't going away. They brought many things that the Indians could use, but they also brought something that no tribe wanted: smallpox. The terrible epidemic that struck the Missouri River tribes in 1837, just a few years before Crazy Horse was born, nearly wiped out the Mandans and drastically weakened the Blackfeet.

The whites came, their disease came, and the game left — not all of it, of course, but even a slight diminution was enough to affect the lives of hunting peoples. Friction steadily increased along the Holy Road; immigrant trains were attacked, the occasional immigrant killed. There was no full-scale warfare yet, just an ominous, continuous rumbling. From the Santa Fe Trail in the south to Fort Union in the north there were clashes, disturbances, apprehension. The Indians, who had at first been friendly with the whites, soon found their patience beginning to fray; the whites, for their part, had never had much patience with the Indians. The Plains Indians were beginning to be seen as mobile impediments; what they stood in the way of was progress, a concept dear to the American politician.

It was to explain this crucial concept — progress — and, by so doing, smooth the way for manifest destiny by speeding the emigrants safely on through to Oregon or California, that the government thought best to convene the great council that was held at Fort Laramie in the summer of 1851. If Crazy Horse was there, which is likely, he was a boy just short of adolescence and was probably drinking in the sights.

There was an abundance of sights to drink in, too. The Fort Laramie council probably drew the greatest assembling of native peoples — or at least, of Plains peoples — prior to the massing at the Little Bighorn a quarter of a century later. I have read many descriptions of the Fort Laramie council, a conclave at which many traditional enemies sat together, but the passage that best suggests the splendor and the wildness of the tribes as they then were is Afric rather than American. Here is Wilfred Thesiger's account of a similar

31

gathering in Addis Ababa in 1916, when his father was British ambassador there:

Each feudal lord was surrounded by levys from the province where he ruled. The simple fighting men were dressed in white but the chiefs wore their full panoply, lion's mane headdresses, brilliant velvet cloaks stiff with silver and golden ornament, long silk robes in many colors and great curved swords. All carried shields, some embossed with silver and gilt, and many carried rifles. The Zulu impis parading before Chaka, or the dervishes drawn up to do battle in front of Omdurman, could have appeared no more barbaric than this frenzied tide of men which surged past the royal pavilion throughout the day, to the thunder of the war drums and the blare of the war horns. This was no ceremonial review. These men had just returned from fighting for their lives, and they were still wild with the excitement of those frantic hours. The blood on the clothes which they had stripped from the dead and draped over their horses was barely dry. They came in waves, horsemen half concealed in dust and a great press of footmen.

Screaming out their deeds of valor and brandishing their weapons they came right up to the steps of the throne. Above them, among glinting spear points, countless banners dipped and waved. . . .

Something rather like this was to occur in Montana, twenty-five years later, on the twenty-fifth of June, 1876. I quote Thesiger not only because he has left a fine description of native splendor, but also because he mentions the Zulus and the dervishes. The Custer battle was only one of the occasions, in the last quarter of the nineteenth century, on which native peoples fought one last victorious fight against the colonizers. Only a little later, on January 27, 1879, twenty thousand Zulus overwhelmed the British garrison at Islandwana, killing thirteen hundred men. In February of 1885 the dervishes overran General Gordon at Khartoum. Geronimo and his eighteen men surrendered in September of 1886, and Sitting Bull was shot and killed by two Indian policemen in the last days of 1890, with the Wounded Knee massacre occurring just afterward.

The great council at Fort Laramie in 1851, which was supposed to mark the end of the United States government's conflict with the Plains Indians, was, in fact, only an especially colorful beginning.

It was an odd beginning, too. There were many highly respected Indian leaders at this council. What immediately became clear — to the Indians, but not to the whites — was that whites and Indians had very different ideas about what a chief was and what powers he might have. All societies have leaders; certainly the Sioux had several of uncommon ability, but rarely did any of them have the direct power of command that was the mark of a "chief" in white culture. The whites had a commander-in-chief who could give orders and expect to have them obeyed. There was, far away, a czar of all the Russias, who had great power over his people; he could also give orders and expect to have them obeyed. The peace commissioners at Fort Laramie seemed to assume that some such leader could be found among the Sioux — a czar of all the Sioux, as it were, and one who, if possible, could boss the Pawnees, the Cheyennes, the Crows, the Shoshones, and the Arapahos as well. This foolish assumption haunted the government's relations with native peoples all through the nineteenth century and well into the twentieth. The Indians had no political mechanism for selecting such a leader, and no intention of obeying him should he appear. That being the case, the whites simply chose for them, passing over the much-respected Old Smoke and settling on an able and sensible Brulé named Conquering Bear (or, sometimes, Whirling Bear).

Having chosen the chief of their choice, the U.S. government agreed to pay the tribes an annuity of $50,000 in goods, for which they expected to get safe passage for immigrants along the Holy Road — peace in their time, as it were. The commissioners went home well satisfied; the Indians divided their presents and went back to their customary lives. No one, of any tribe, had any intention of obeying Conquering Bear, unless his wish happened to coincide with what they wanted. They may not even have understood that the whites harbored such a foolish expectation. Conquering Bear may have supposed that he was now chief of the Brulés, and possibly, at a stretch, of the Oglalas, but even of the Oglalas he would have been far from sure. As for being chief of all the Sioux, much less of all the Plains Indians — well, that was a ridiculous notion that no one took seriously. There was no chief of all the

Sioux — never had been, never would be.

Perhaps the most interesting thing to come out of the Fort Laramie council was the government's misreading of what chieftaincy meant among the Plains Indians. They could not rid themselves of the expectation that a Sioux or a Cheyenne or a Pawnee, once called a chief, would then begin to behave exactly like a white CEO, bossing people around, initiating, restraining. They were unprepared to recognize that Indian societies didn't work that way. The Sioux were highly individualistic people; though they often acted in concert on hunts and raids, at other times each man simply went his own way. Crazy Horse ignored the sundance, spent a lot of time by himself, raided when he wanted to. If he could find a few warriors willing to go raiding with him, that was fine; but if no one in camp was in a martial mood, he went alone.

The issue of chieftaincy remains ticklish because, through long usage, most of those who read about the Plains Indians, and some of those who write about them, come to assume that the Indians who proved most successful in councils and parleys with the whites were really chiefs back home, when in many cases they were not, Red Cloud being a famous example. The struggle for the Bozeman Trail and the Powder River country is often called Red Cloud's war, and he is commonly thought to have won that war when the government closed three forts in 1868. But many of the Sioux who knew him were merely amused by the notion that Red Cloud was a chief, although they did concede that personally he was valorous enough. But he didn't sit in the council of elders and wise men called the Big Bellies. The Sioux may have noticed problems with Red Cloud's character — vanity, for example — that escaped the whites, for a time, though they certainly didn't escape agent Valentine McGillycuddy, who had a long and bitter struggle with him in the years after Crazy Horse's death. Red Cloud's name is on the plaque at the Fetterman battlefield, though several authorities doubt that he fought in that battle; nor was he at the Little Bighorn, though in extreme old age he seems to have believed that he was.

The whites decided Red Cloud was a big chief because he was able in dealing with *them*. He was prominent in many parleys and conferences, went to Washington several times, and even made a speech at Cooper Union, in New York City, in 1870.

Red Cloud and Spotted Tail both recognized quickly that the whites were too powerful to oppose directly — much too powerful. Whatever might be said in the parleys, and whatever was written on the papers, the whites meant to win; they were going to take what they wanted, which, in the end, was all the country that the native peoples had once inhabited. Red Cloud may not have been a big chief to his own people, but he had, early on, made a true reckoning of white ability and white intent. The bottom line, for Red Cloud, was that the whites were going to take it all. Thus, in the big council of 1874, over the Black Hills, where gold had been discovered by the ubiquitous General Custer, Red Cloud advocated selling, and for a big price. Clearly the whites were going to take the Black Hills anyway — why not get some money and a lot of goods?

This council in 1874 was the one to which Crazy Horse — who attended no councils — may have sent Little Big Man as his representative. Little Big Man (the Sioux warrior, not the character in Thomas Berger's novel) raced into the company almost naked, announcing that he would shoot anyone who wanted to sell the Black Hills. Red Cloud had just been about to launch into one of his stem-winding orations when Little Big Man arrived. Sitting Bull was a reluctant parleyer, but Crazy Horse went him one better: he just didn't parley — not until 1877, when he finally came in. Before that he stayed away, amid his caves and holes, which is one reason so much of his life is simply a mystery. But this avoidance of parleys may also have meant that he never made the kind of hardheaded assessment of white character and white intentions that Red Cloud, Spotted Tail, and Sitting Bull arrived at early on.

4

What Crazy Horse did learn about whites while still quite young was the destructive force of their caprice. This knowledge came to him because of the famous incident of the Mormon cow (or, possibly, the Mormon ox). As usual, we can date the incident — August 17, 1854 — only because a lot of white people got killed, thirty-one this time.

Conquering Bear, the Brulé leader whom the whites had hoped to make the czar of all the Sioux, was living, along with some Minniconjous and some Oglalas, near the camp of Old Smoke, the much-respected Sioux leader, when a party of Mormons came through, one of them driving a lame cow. The Sioux camp was not far from Fort Laramie. The lame cow wandered through this camp and a Minniconjou warrior named High Forehead (or Straight Foretop) killed her. Many immigrant trains passed over the Holy Road that summer, and the young Sioux warriors pestered them, nipping a cow here and a horse there. Some of their prizes were a good deal more to be desired than this lame cow.

Despite the poor quality of the animal, the Mormon owner didn't take his loss lightly. He complained at Fort Laramie, and the young commander of the force there unwisely chose this lame cow as an excuse for attempting to bring the Sioux to heel. The officer, Lieutenant Hugh Fleming, summoned Conquering Bear, and Conquering Bear did his best to mollify both the army and the irate Mormon. He even offered to let the Mormon visit his horse herd and pick out a fine pony to replace his crippled cow. But Lieutenant Fleming, backed up by the equally hotheaded Lieutenant John Grattan, refused this sensible compromise. Fleming demanded that Conquering Bear — in his eyes a supreme leader — surrender High Forehead. Conquering Bear pointed out that High Forehead was a Minniconjou; no Brulé had the authority to order his arrest.

There were only about one hundred soldiers in Fort Laramie at this time, and well over a thousand Sioux in the vicinity, which didn't stop the impatient, Indian-hating Grattan from dragging some artillery off to the Sioux village, with which to

42

back up his demand for High Forehead's arrest.

What occurred then was what usually occurred when a white military unit was wiped out by a native force: casual and contemptuous underestimation, on the part of the whites, of native skill and will. Lieutenant Grattan came into the Sioux village with thirty-one men and an interpreter named Wyuse, who had not helped matters by putting an insulting spin on Conquering Bear's dignified remarks to Lieutenant Fleming. High Forehead stood in plain sight but was not disposed to be arrested, whereupon Lieutenant Grattan shot off his cannon, missing most of the village but mortally wounding Conquering Bear, the man who had been, throughout, the voice of moderation and good sense. High Forehead shot Lieutenant Grattan and the thirty-one soldiers were immediately massacred, along with Wyuse, who was dealt with with extreme prejudice by the outraged Sioux. The Sioux — who could probably have overrun Fort Laramie had they chosen to — took Conquering Bear onto the Plains, far away from whites, so that he could die and be buried in the traditional Sioux way. They melted into the prairies, buried their good leader, and went on with life.

Various historians have chided the Sioux for not fighting as, say, West Pointers fought, but that was not their way. To them tribal warfare, though starkly violent, was nothing like as generally deadly as the forces whites would soon loose against one another in their own Civil War. In a sense every Sioux was his own general, attacking when he wanted to attack, retreating when the odds seemed too long or the weather too bad. Consider this description of tribal warfare, as observed by Peter Matthiessen in New Guinea in the early 1960s and recorded in *Under the Mountain Wall*:

At the north end of the Tokolik there is an open meadow. Here the main body of the Kurelu were gathering. Over one hundred had now appeared, and at a signal a group of these now ran down the hill toward the reedy pool. On the far bank a party of Wittaia danced and called. The enemies shouted insults at each other and brandished spears, but no arrows flew and shortly both sides retired to their rear positions.

The sun had climbed over the valley and its light shone on breastplates of white sheels, on white headdresses, on ivory boar's tusks inserted through nostrils, on wands of white egret feathers twirled like batons. The shouting was increasing in ferocity, and several men from each side would dance out and feign attacks, whirling and prancing to display their splendor. They were jeered and admired by both sides and were not shot at, for display and panoply were a part of war, which was less war than ceremonial sport, a wild fierce festival. Territorial conquest was unknown to the akuni; there was land enough for all, and at the end of the day the warriors would go home across the fields to supper. Should rain come to chill them or spoil their feathers, both sides would retire. A day of war was dangerous and splendid, regardless of its outcome; it was a war of individuals and gallantry, quite innocent of tactics and cold slaughter. A single death on either side would mean victory or defeat.

Toward mid-morning a flurry of arrows was exchanged . . . soon a great shout rose up out of the distance, and the Kurelu answered it exultantly, hoo-ah, hoo-ah-h, hua hua, hua. . . .

Add horses and you get something not

very unlike what the Sioux did when they went out on a day's raiding. Once the two sides faced off, there would be lots of shouting, taunting, feints, dashes, with now and then an injury and now and then a death, after which, tribal honor having been defended and acts of individual bravery performed and witnessed, everyone yelled a few more times and went home. (There were some serious battles and even a few massacres, but these were the exceptions, not the norm.)

Crazy Horse fought in many raids of this sort; seldom would more than a man or two be killed in such forays. A desire to steal horses was usually the nominal aim of Plains warfare, but the need for the warriors — young warriors, particularly — to display their bravery was usually the real motive.

Not long after the Grattan massacre, Crazy Horse, who was then living with his mother's people, the Brulés, rode off alone to seek a vision, ignoring the rituals and procedures of purification that would normally precede a vision quest. He felt that he needed a vision and simply rode off to seek it, across the prairies of what is now western Nebraska. To have done this right he would have had to fast, be purified in a sweat lodge, and perhaps be given a lecture or two by a holy man — his father, for example. But orthodoxy was not his way, would never be his way. When Crazy Horse felt like doing something, he just did it.

Perhaps because he didn't fully prepare himself for this vision quest, he only achieved what to him at the time seemed a rather mediocre vision. Such a vision was supposed to put a young man in touch with the eternal, with the sacred powers; properly interpreted, the vision would help him find what we now call identity, and thus show him what was to be his way in life. His vision, correctly understood, would be determinative, give him direction, show him what he must do and how he must behave.

The vision Crazy Horse (then still called Curly) achieved, after fasting alone for two days, has been variously reported. It seems he dreamed of a horseman, floating above the ground. The horseman was dressed plainly, was not painted, was in no way grand; the horse may have been dancing, or in some way magical. The horseman told Crazy Horse not to adorn himself, not to wear a war bonnet; he was permitted a single feather at most. He was instructed to throw a little dust over his horse before going into battle, and to wear a small stone behind his ear. There may have been a battle in the vision, a battle in which the horseman had his arms held by one of his own people. But neither bullets nor arrows touched him. The horseman told Crazy Horse *never* to keep anything for himself.

Shortly after the dream ended, his father found him. His friend Hump had also come looking for him. They had been worried about him because both Crows and Pawnees were known to have been in the area. His father, a shaman after all, was outraged that his son had simply gone riding off on a vision quest, without making the proper preparation, endangering himself in the process. He let his son know that he had committed a serious violation of custom. Crazy Horse probably kept quiet about his rather low-rent vision for a while, until his father was over his pique; but eventually Worm did find out about the dream and did interpret it. Dreaming, dream reporting, and dream interpretation were an important part of Sioux life. The Sioux sought guidance from dreams as intently as did the patients of Dr. Freud, though of course through different methods and with different results.

According to most reports, about two years passed before Crazy Horse revealed his dream to his father. This time the two went off together, fasted, built a sweat lodge, did it right. His father listened and confirmed the horseman's instructions: Crazy Horse was to dress simply, put a small stone behind his ear, and, most important, he was not to keep anything for himself. Instead, he was to be a man of charity, doing his best to feed the poor and helpless members of the tribe.

His duty to the poor was a duty that Crazy Horse took seriously all his life — it may have been because he doubted his ability to feed the many hungry people who were following him that he decided to bring the band into Fort Robinson in 1877.

The other element in the dream that has acquired the force of legend is that Crazy Horse could be injured only if one of his own people held his arms. On one crucial occasion (perhaps two) a member of his own people *did* hold his arms; on another occasion he forgot his instructions and kept something for himself — specifically, two Arapaho scalps — and was promptly injured in the leg.

If we have received this dream accurately

across one hundred and forty-five years, it would seem that Crazy Horse followed its precepts as best he could, although, being human, he slipped in a couple of instances, as we shall see. But he always dressed plainly; he threw dust on himself and his horse before going into battle; he wore a single feather and put a small stone behind his ear. When he painted at all, it was only with a zigzag representing lightning and perhaps a few white spots representing hail or snow. Many commentators who saw him in his years of battle mention the simplicity of his dress. When he brought his band into the fort in 1877, He Dog and the other warriors were in full panoply — one soldier said it didn't look like a surrender, it looked like a triumphal march — but Crazy Horse dressed as simply as ever. Through all the difficulties of his life he seems to have remained true to the conditions laid down in his dream, although he had considered it a poor dream at the time.

5

The U.S. government, meanwhile, during the most intense years of warfare with the Plains Indians, pursued a carrot-and-stick policy that was consistent only in its inconsistency. The army almost always underestimated Indian ability, and then, when they were whipped through some foolish action of their own — as with Grattan — they just as invariably overreacted. Every white military defeat from Grattan to the Custer battle came because some white commander arrogantly supposed that he could whip any number of Indians, on any field at any time. When this stupid assumption was disproven, the army, or in some cases, such irregulars as could be pulled together, reacted by punishing whatever Indians they could catch, whether they had taken part in a particular attack or not.

Thus the fate of the wise and considerate Cheyenne leader Black Kettle, a peace Indian from the start. Black Kettle first had his village riddled by Chivington at Sand Creek, and then had it riddled again by Custer on the Washita, in 1868, even though up at Fort Laramie Red Cloud had just signed a major peace treaty.

At this juncture the two military systems, white and Sioux, suffered from similar elements of unpredictability, especially where their young warriors were concerned. Though Black Kettle was for peace, his young men could not always be restrained, and neither could young white men such as Custer. No Plains Indian ever completely controlled the young warriors, except briefly, nor did any white leader long control George Armstrong Custer.

About a year after the Grattan massacre near Fort Laramie (1854), the army finally got up a punitive expedition against the Sioux, although the Sioux involved in the massacre — Brulés, mainly — were by then scattered here and there across the prairies. An expedition of about six hundred men under General W. S. Harney (the Sioux were to call him Mad Bear) set out to avenge Grattan. At first they found no Sioux to punish. Six hundred men was a huge force; nothing like Harney's army had yet been seen on the northern plains. Nobody was expecting it — many Sioux bands were unaware that a large body of white men were marching across the prairie, out for their blood. Some did know, because runners had gone out to the tribes, telling them that the U.S. government wanted them south of the Platte River; those who didn't go would be considered hostile. Many Sioux bands *were* south of the Platte, but the Brulés weren't, and neither were the Minniconjous.

General Harney, after considerable frustration, finally located the village of Little Thunder, a Brulé headman then camped on the banks of the Bluewater River. There had been a good hunt; the women of the village were busy working the buffalo hides.

Little Thunder knew the soldiers were coming — it would have been hard not to know it — but he seemed to have disregarded whatever warning he received. When the soldiers arrived, there was some parleying, but only because General Harney wanted to get his troops into position. When he *had* them in position, he proceeded to destroy Little Thunder's village, killing nearly ninety Indians in a few minutes and taking many captives. Spotted Tail fought in this battle and never forgot the carnage he witnessed that day.

It is thought that Crazy Horse was living with Little Thunder that summer, but was out hunting when the terrible attack came. This may be the sort of rumor that makes Crazy Horse a kind of Zelig, turning up wherever the action is. Spotted Tail was so awed by the power of white weaponry that he later came to Fort Laramie and turned himself in; he served two years in jail and was probably the first of the major Sioux leaders to conclude that the Sioux could not hope to win in sustained conflict with the whites.

Most authorities think that Crazy Horse came back to what had been Little Thunder's village, saw the carnage, and rescued a young Cheyenne maiden called Yellow Woman; he took her back to her people and began what was to be a long and friendly association with the Cheyennes.

With his easy victory on the Bluewater, General Harney, Mad Bear, had essentially won control of the Platte River and the Oregon Trail. The war for the northern plains was just beginning, but this was a significant victory nonetheless. That the whites were willing, almost casually, to destroy a whole village was a new fact that the Sioux would have to come to terms with. In the warfare between tribes such a thing did not happen; there was no such imbalance of weaponry. The scorched-earth policy that General Sherman was to pursue so effectively a few years later — warfare as terror — hadn't come to the west, or anywhere else, at this time. The carnage at the Bluewater was the closest thing to it. Spotted Tail, who saw that carnage close up, from then on believed that the whites could wipe out the Sioux whenever they chose to.

Throughout Crazy Horse's life, he, like all the other Plains Indians, would have to grapple with a too-rapid pace of change. The Sioux and the Cheyennes and the other tribes still hunted buffalo, in the main, with bows and arrows. In their warfare they had bows, lances, clubs, tomahawks, etc. They knew about guns, of course, but only a few had firearms at this time. That the whites could use guns so effectively as to kill ninety Sioux in a few minutes was a new thing. Crazy Horse, whether he saw the destruction at the Bluewater or merely heard about it, spent the rest of his life either avoiding whites or fighting them.

He would have preferred, I imagine, simply to avoid them and go on living a traditional Sioux life, raiding, hunting, dreaming; but the option of avoidance was not available to him for very long. The whites were too many, and they weren't satisfied with the Holy Road. They weren't satisfied with any one place or one road; they wanted everything. So he fought: on the Bozeman, on the Powder River, on the Yellowstone, in the Black Hills, on the Tongue and the Rosebud, at the Little Bighorn. He was a participant and possibly a catalyst at three of the Indians' greatest victories: Fetterman, the Rosebud, the Little Bighorn. He didn't win the war. What is hard to judge is how long he really expected to, if he ever expected to. Despite much urging, and unlike Red Cloud, Spotted Tail, and Sitting Bull, he never went east, never saw the whites in their seats of power; had he done so, he might have drawn the same conclusion they drew. But he went his own way, traveled his own road, until it dead-ended at Fort Robinson in September of 1877. Looked back on from the perspective of one hundred and twenty years, his doom seems Sophoclean, inevitable; but perhaps all dooms do, once the roads taken and not taken deliver the character to his fate.

6

By most accounts, Crazy Horse spent the winter of 1856–57 with Yellow Woman's people, in Kansas. Young Man Afraid, son of the much-respected Old Man Afraid, was with him; the son would one day be much respected too. It may have been about this time that a Cheyenne medicine man convinced the young warriors that he had a medicine so strong that it would turn away bullets, a belief that has surfaced frequently among native peoples. The Comanche prophet Isatai convinced Quanah Parker and others that bullets would not harm them, whereupon they attacked some buffalo hunters who were securely forted up in the old trading post called Adobe Walls. Alas, the bullets proved easily able to penetrate both the medicine and the Comanches, perhaps because a warrior spoiled it by riding a mule rather than a horse. The dervishes believed themselves to be bulletproof when they lined up to be slaughtered at Omdurman; and the belief has cropped up again in Africa within recent decades.

But the young Sioux and Cheyennes in Kansas in the summer of 1857 never got to put this strong magic to a test. They ran into a party of soldiers and prepared to attack, but the soldiers, indifferent to whether the Sioux were bulletproof or not, charged them with drawn sabers. The Sioux may have thought themselves bulletproof, but they knew they weren't saberproof, so they fled — an embarrassing rout.

Later that summer several thousand Indians gathered at Bear Butte to parley — ineffectively, as it proved — about the whites. Crazy Horse was probably there, with his friend Hump; it may have been at this gathering that he met Touch-the-Clouds, the seven-foot Minniconjou warrior who attended him in his last hour.

Also, it may have been at this large conclave that Crazy Horse met the woman who was to be the love of his life: Black Buffalo Woman, one of Red Cloud's nieces. It was because of his great, irrepressible passion for Black Buffalo Woman that he was later to fail in his grave responsibility to the tribe, once he had been given the high honor of being made a Shirt-wearer, a story we will get to in good time.

This parley at Bear Butte in the end changed nothing. There was general agreement that the tribes needed to take a sterner line with the whites, before their hunting grounds were completely destroyed; but how exactly they were to do that, with each band moving along with the game and looking essentially to their own needs, was hard to say. The whites had a great advantage: they were one nation (though soon to be split, temporarily); the native peoples of the plains were many nations.

The bitter lesson all the Plains Indians had to begin to absorb in the late 1850s was how very quickly nature's abundance — that is, game — could become scarcity. The hunting along the Platte was already much diminished; the great masses of buffalo upon which all the tribes were dependent had by then been split into a northern and a southern herd. The hard fighting between Brulé Sioux and Pawnee, which so occupied Spotted Tail, was intensified by the fact that the two peoples were competing for a dwindling supply of game.

For the Oglalas, the same need to stay where the game was abundant forced them west and north and brought increased conflict with the tribes already there, namely, the Arapahos, the Shoshones, and the Crows.

It was on a raid against the Arapahos,

probably in the summer of 1858, that Crazy Horse — he would have then been about sixteen — finally earned his name. He charged straight at a party of enemy warriors, untouched by either arrows or bullets; his bravery was so exceptional that the Sioux began to sing in his honor. When two Arapaho warriors rode out to challenge him, he killed both of them and took their scalps, forgetting in the heat of battle that his dream had told him never to keep anything for himself. While he was taking the scalps, he was hit in the leg by an arrow. He threw the scalps away and his friend Hump removed the arrow and treated the wound. When the Oglalas returned to their camp, old Crazy Horse, the father, made a fine ceremony and transferred the name to his son. Thereafter the old man was called Worm and Crazy Horse took the name by which history knows him.

These were not his first kills. Sometime earlier, in a skirmish with some Omahas, he shot at what he thought was a warrior, crouched in some bushes, and discovered that he had killed a woman. He did not take this scalp.

In the main the Oglala effort to edge into the game-rich Powder River country was successful.

The years of Crazy Horse's early manhood were years of relative prosperity for the Sioux; one reason for this was that the whites were soon fighting a terrible civil war, a war so destructive that, by contrast, their conflicts with the Plains Indians seemed almost like frolics. From 1861 to 1865 the army had all it could handle elsewhere; the best officers, naturally, wanted to fight in that fight, leaving the western forts ill manned, usually by officers who resented the fact that they weren't fighting the Rebs. Some very ugly incidents — for one, the great Sioux uprising in Minnesota in 1862 — took place during the Civil War; but farther west, where Crazy Horse was, the fighting during these years was mainly Indian against Indian. It was in these years that Crazy Horse earned the high reputation among his fellow Indians that he would carry all the way to the Little Bighorn.

7

It is perhaps appropriate to pause during this nominal lull in the plains warfare — nominal because there was never a total cessation of hostilities — to say a word about the plains themselves: this great American steppe was Crazy Horse's home during his whole life. His attachment to these plains never weakened; he was born to those great skies and those long horizons, and he kept to them as long as he could. When Nelson A. Miles attacked him and his people in their winter camp on the Tongue River in January of 1877, Crazy Horse knew that the terms of the conflict had changed. For the Sioux, warfare was mainly a summer sport. In the hard northern winters they had enough to do just to keep their old and their young warm and well fed. It is true that they wiped out Fetterman on a cold day in December, accomplishing that task just before a blizzard struck, but, in the main, winter warfare was not something they enjoyed. Fighting was a great deal more pleasant in warm weather.

Bearcoat Miles came anyway, and kept coming, forcing Crazy Horse to make an awkward and painful retreat. Then the winter stopped even General Miles; and Crazy Horse, in the breather it allowed him, had the opportunity to do what Chief Joseph had hoped to do and what Sitting Bull *did* do: escape into Canada. Neither Miles nor Crook could have followed him there; the Canadian government would not have tolerated it, although, almost a decade later, Crook found the Mexican government far more pliant when he went in after Geronimo.

Crazy Horse refused to go to Canada. It was even colder in Canada, and the game was uncertain; but it may be that he didn't go because he refused to be chased from his home country. The range that he traveled in his life was spacious, but it wasn't infinite. He went south a few times into Kansas, west as far as the Bighorn Mountains, north and east to the Missouri country; but the land where he roamed and fought mainly was plains country: Nebraska, Wyoming, South Dakota, eastern Montana. Rarely if ever was he east of the 100th meridian, that important line on the map that told the whites where the Great American Desert began.

It wasn't desert, of course — Geronimo lived in a desert. Crazy Horse lived near the center of the great grassland steppe that stretched from Texas well into Canada. Then and now, the central plains were the least populated part of the United States. To those not attuned to their subtleties the plains are merely monotonous emptiness. But to those who love them, the plains are endlessly fascinating, a place where the constant interplay of land and sky is always dramatic; gloomy sometimes, but more often uplifting. Despite their unpopularity with the general public, many writers have penned rhapsodies to the plains, and the eyes of many artists — from Catlin and Bodmer on — have been challenged by them.

The American plains, like all the world's great steppes, are the natural home for grazing animals and nomadic peoples, and are particularly ideal for certain large ruminants such as the buffalo. The plains have never welcomed either the plow or the fence. The balance of the grasses, the wildlife, and the climate is delicate, easily disturbed. Not merely Crazy Horse but all the Plains Indians recognized with dismay that the whites were indifferent to this balance and likely to destroy it.

Nomads, of course, can be wanton too; like most humans they are inclined to the binge. But, in the main, they held a sacramental attitude toward the earth and its creatures, whereas the white attitude from the first was essentially commercial.

Nomadic lifestyles are often vulnerable to the technologies of settled people; and yet the appeal of what appears to be freedom — the freedom of the nomad, whether Sioux Indian or lone cowboy — remains very potent. It may be that one reason writers from the American west have had such a hard time getting their words taken seriously is that they have been competing from the first with one of the most powerful visual images of all: the image of horses running. The Indian and the horse have been together in movies for as long as there have been movies: I now own a tape of a fragmentary silent film called *Old Texas*, made in 1913, in which the great cattleman Charles Goodnight appears briefly at a picnic before the film — possibly it is supposed to represent his reminiscences — dissolves into grainy images of Indians on horses.

Crazy Horse was not unaware of mountains. He knew the Bighorns and the Black Hills, was born near and died not far from

Bear Butte. But for most of his life he was a man of the Great Plains. His rivers were the Platte, the Niobrara, the Powder, the Yellowstone, the Tongue, the Little Missouri. He lived under one of the most generous skies in the world. Again, many commentators have recognized that such skies, hovering over the rolling land, with the horizons a mystery, with mirages frequent, make the plains a place that calls forth imaginings. Those long vistas, those splendid clouds tempt the imagination as the plains of Castile tempted Don Quixote. When Plains people die, white or Indian, they speak of a going up, for where would the spirit go except into that sky? It is easy on the plains to imagine things not seen, worlds not known. Crazy Horse, in his wanderings over the summer plains, would have seen many mirages, which perhaps encouraged him in his belief that this world, with its buffalo and horses, is only the shadow of the real world. He was in a way a prairie Platonist, seeing an ideal of which the day's events were only a shadow. His belief in the two worlds seems to have made him exceptionally cautious where the camera is concerned. He didn't want any white man to snatch his shadow, coax it into a little box. He wouldn't even allow his friend Dr. McGillycuddy, the doctor who so faithfully treated his wife Black Shawl for tuberculosis, to take his picture. He believed it would shorten his life; and his life did indeed end not long after he came to the place where cameras — the little boxes that snatched shadows — were common.

This strange man of the Oglalas was always a man of the central plains. He would not be driven from them, rejecting, in a crucial decision, even the plains of Canada. He was determined to hold to the country that was his own, and in the end, that is what he did.

8

While the whites were busy in the east, fighting one another, Crazy Horse was active in the old way, harassing his enemies, stealing horses, hunting, sharing what he killed with the poor and helpless, and, it seems, yearning for a woman he couldn't have.

This was the same fetching young woman he had probably spotted at the big council in 1857: Black Buffalo Woman. She was young and comely — his was hardly the only eye to fall on her, but for a time Crazy Horse seemed to feel that he was at least in the running for her affections. One day he left on a raid with several warriors, one of whom, No Water, soon developed such a terrible toothache that he dropped out of the raiding party and went back to camp. When the raid ended, Crazy Horse discovered to his extreme dismay that in his absence Black Buffalo Woman had married No Water. (Some believe the match was engineered by Red Cloud, the girl's uncle.)

Crazy Horse took this news hard, as any young man in love would be apt to. He was perhaps twenty-one or twenty-two at the time and had been hanging out almost exclusively in the camp of the Bad Faces (the girl's people, and also Red Cloud's). Crazy Horse left the camp at once and was gone for some time.

Black Buffalo Woman had made her choice, and that should have been the end of it, but it wasn't. Crazy Horse was an unusually single-minded young man; Black Buffalo Woman happened to be the only woman he had serious feelings for. These feelings didn't go away, although Black Buffalo Woman was a respectable wife and, soon, a mother. Other young warriors took wives: Crazy Horse didn't. Instead he hung around No Water's lodge as much as possible. No Water, as it turned out, was a jealous husband. He was not pleased when Crazy Horse continued to pay his wife little attentions, but he tolerated the situation. For some years, while Black Buffalo Woman bore No Water three children, a reasonable decorum was observed.

Around 1865, just as the long Civil War between the whites was ending, the Oglala Sioux revived the old custom of the Shirt-wearers. The Oglala society of elders, sometimes called the Big Bellies and sometimes called other names, sat down and chose four young men of proven courage and good moral character and honored them by making them Shirt-wearers. Their duty, from then on, was to put selfish interests aside and think always of the welfare of the tribe. Those duties were as much moral as practical; they were, in our terms, to be role models, to set examples of how Sioux men should behave. The Big Bellies themselves had not been formally elected; they were just there to advise and counsel, to plan hunts, to decide when to move their camp, and so on.

Crazy Horse, as has been noted, was not from one of the great families of the Sioux. His father was a poor man, a healer, a reader of dreams.

Young Man Afraid *was* of such a great family. His father, Old Man Afraid, was, in a way, the tribe's senior diplomat. When the Shirt-wearer ceremony was revived, Young Man Afraid was chosen first, and then American Horse, Sword, and Crazy Horse. This was a very great honor, one that put Crazy Horse in a position of grave responsibility. He was chosen both for his courage and for his charity, his concern for the weak ones. He was expected to keep little for himself, which was no problem; since the time of his dream he had never kept much for himself. The problem was that he was a single man: he hadn't married.

Though the Civil War had drawn off much of the force of the white military, there was no agreed-upon peace on the prairies. The Santee Sioux rose up in Minnesota, and the Sioux along the Missouri River harried the soldiers when there were any to harry. The Shoshones still made things difficult for immigrants along the Holy Road. In Texas the Comanches and the Kiowas rebounded somewhat and kept pressure on the settlers' frontier; in Kansas the Cheyennes fought white soldiers when they met them, and so on. It was mainly the Teton Sioux who could, during this period, enjoy good hunting in relative peace. This was largely because of where they were, west of Fort Laramie and south of the Yellowstone River, an area full of game and almost empty of whites. This period of relative ease they owed in part to the wisdom of Old Man Afraid, who believed, with Sitting Bull, that it was best to stay away from the whites as long as it was possible to do so. Still, even then, the rush of immigrants along the Holy Road was constant, and the game, in consequence, harder to find and kill. This irritant was powerful enough that the northern and southern Sioux and some Cheyennes made plans to act in concert; the big offensive they planned to mount would start in the north, with Sitting Bull attacking Fort Rice.

To the extent that this was ever a fully planned offensive, it fizzled for the usual reasons. The older men, the tacticians, could never get the young warriors to wait. The force Crazy Horse may have been with, perhaps as many as one thousand warriors, chose to hit the spot where the Oregon Trail crosses the North Platte River, at what is called the Platte River Bridge. The huge party of Sioux should have been able to surprise and overwhelm the troopers guarding the bridge at the time, but they couldn't and went home disappointed, having killed only a few whites. This battle (July 25, 1864) had one especially sad death. A young lieutenant named Caspar Collins, who was very friendly with the Sioux and had camped with them on several occasions, was killed late in the fight, possibly because his horse bolted and carried him straight into a group of Cheyennes, who immediately did him in. Had Caspar Collins lived, he might have been able to tell us something of Crazy Horse — it is believed the two knew one another. But either because of an uncontrollable horse, or because he allowed himself to be lured into a trap by the Cheyenne decoys, the young lieutenant lost his life.

In 1865 the U.S. government's Indian policy was at its most schizophrenic. The nation as a whole was war-weary, weighted with grief, and, after President Lincoln's assassination, a little addled. The nascent peace party wanted to buy off the hostile Indians, give them money and good land — though never *much* good land — if they would behave; at the same time the military wanted to send a big bunch of soldiers to punish them for their temerity in not immediately accepting the white man's way. Unable to decide between peace and war, the government tried both at once. They sent out a bunch of soldiers to punish any hostiles they could find, while at the same time hastily convening a peace conference whose aim was to secure something like squatter's rights to the Platte River country. The large troop of soldiers found no Indians in any numbers and hunted so poorly that they sometimes had to eat their horses, whereas the peace conference attracted only ration Indians who exercised no control over the Platte River country, or, indeed, any country.

Back east, though, at least one indubitably good thing had happened: the Civil War ended. Having failed to sign up any hostiles at the little peace conference in 1865, the government tried another in 1866. Gold had been discovered in Montana, and soon a flood of miners were seeking the quickest way to it, which happened to be by a route that became known as the Bozeman Trail.

Again the government, whether it fully realized it or not, set about pursuing peace and war at once. General Sherman, aggressive as ever, wanted to immediately start building forts along the Bozeman Trail. So far the Sioux had been quiet, even letting most of the miners go through: perhaps Sherman thought he could get away with two or three forts. He sent Colonel Henry Carrington and a sizable force into the Powder River country to get the fort building started. At the same time the Indian Office called a peace conference at Fort Laramie, and this time Red Cloud and some of the other headmen came in to hear what the white men had to offer. Perhaps the peace commissioners hoped that they would have a deal concluded before the Sioux happened to notice Carrington and his troops on the plain by the Powder River, but they were not to be so lucky. A Brulé named Standing Elk ran into Carrington and was casually informed of the plan to build the forts. Standing Elk loped over to Fort Laramie to pass on this news, arriving just in time to provoke one of Red Cloud's most dramatic exits. Neither he nor the other Sioux leaders were pleased with the news that the whites were already preparing to apply the stick when they themselves had just made a long trip to talk about carrots. No signatures were obtained — at least not the right ones — and for the next couple of years the Bozeman Trail was one of the most hotly contested routes in the west. The gold was in Montana, the money to mine it was in the east, and in between were some very angry Indians who by this time had had enough of being pushed around by the whites.

As a consequence of Sherman's initiative in fort building, one of the most famous and immediately pertinent comeuppances in Plains Indian warfare was visited on Captain William Fetterman and his unfortunate troop on the twenty-first of December, 1866. Fetterman, by all accounts, was a frustrated young officer who had the misfortune to be stationed at Fort Phil Kearney under the unconcerned, even lackadaisical, command of Colonel Carrington. Fetterman considered Carrington to be what we would now call a wimp or a wuss. Though three forts were to be stuck in the very heart of Sioux country, Carrington showed no inclination to make war on the Indians. No treaties had been signed, no presents exchanged, and there existed no hope of peace along the Bozeman; but it was left to Captain Fetterman to reap the whirlwind that his superiors had called up.

Fetterman was an arrogant young man who had no regard for Indians; he had publicly said that with eighty men he could march through the whole Sioux nation. On that cold December day he got his chance. He demanded that Carrington let him lead a troop of men in the defense of some woodcutters who were being harassed by a few Indians. Carrington consented, but with reluctance. He would have preferred to send a more reliable officer, but finally yielded to Fetterman's demands — though he made it clear that on no account was Fetterman to follow the Indians over Lodge Trail Ridge.

Captain Fetterman, having bullied his

way into the assignment, rode out of the fort with eighty men, the very number he had said he could ride through the whole Sioux nation with. The Sioux and the Cheyennes, in large numbers, had been waiting with uncharacteristic patience, hoping a sizable group of soldiers would expose themselves. For once, the young warriors refrained from spoiling the ambush. Crazy Horse led a party of decoys whose job it was to tempt the soldiers to go where they had been told *not* to go: over Lodge Trail Ridge, a move that would take them out of sight of the fort.

The soldiers, of course, were no strangers to the decoy tactics; they were not easily tempted. The legend is that it was Crazy Horse who skillfully and successfully played the wounded bird, leading the soldiers farther and farther from safety. He dismounted several times, pretending that his horse was lame; at one point he even built a small fire. Captain Fetterman had not insisted on taking this command merely to protect a few woodcutters. Eventually, ignoring his strict orders, he took the bait, led his soldiers over Lodge Trail Ridge, and went down the other side. The Indians, in this instance perfectly disciplined, sprang the trap: in half an hour or less Captain Fetterman and his eighty men were dead. By some accounts Captain Fetterman saved his last bullet for himself; American Horse, however, claimed that he clubbed him down and cut his throat. Red Cloud, who probably wasn't there himself, later said that he couldn't remember American Horse being there. There were so many arrows in the air at the same time that some of the Indians may have been wounded by what we now call friendly fire.

Whether Red Cloud was present at this battle remains a matter for debate. Stanley Vestal thinks he wasn't, but George Hyde believes he was somewhere around, being a general of sorts. Crazy Horse had his reputation enhanced, but the victory was somewhat spoiled for him by the death of his friend Lone Bear. The soldiers in Fort Phil Kearney expected to be attacked that night, but the Indians faded into a winter blizzard.

General Sherman, like everyone else, underestimated the fighting spirit of the Plains Indians and misjudged their determination to resist the utter destruction of the hunting grounds upon which they depended. Sherman had the peace party to contend with, and an underabundance of funds besides. The railroads which would eventually bracket the Sioux were on their way but not yet far enough west to be decisive.

The Sioux and the Cheyennes hacked up the bodies of Fetterman and his men in a terrible but customary fashion. Some of the Cheyennes probably remembered that Chivington's men had done exactly the same thing to Black Kettle's people at Sand Creek. The Indians vented their fury on corpses; this is likely to occur in every war — think of Bosnia — but when these mutilations were reported in the eastern newspapers, they had the usual inflammatory effect on the nonmilitary public. It was, however, a divided public. The likelihood is that the government *could* have bought off most of the hostile Indians if they had offered adequate monies and decently spacious reservations. But the government was invariably penny-pinching in its allocations, and much of what it did allot was immediately siphoned off by corrupt Indian agents. Sherman, in charge of a large and unwieldy district, was for a time helpless. He could not put enough men in the field to scorch the vast earth of the west, while the money that could then be offered for peace did not impress hardheaded negotiators such as Red Cloud and

Spotted Tail. If they were going to sell their patrimony for goods, they wanted fine goods, not tacky goods.

The strategic flaws in the military approach were demonstrated conclusively in 1867 when General Hancock led a large and well-publicized expedition into the central plains, accomplishing almost nothing. This lumbering force annoyed the southern Cheyennes, who had not been causing much trouble at the time. George Armstrong Custer had some fun shooting buffalo along the Smoky Hill River, but very few Indians were fought or even seen. This campaign was such an embarrassing failure that the army, for a time, gave up on a military solution to the problem of the Plains Indians. It was once again demonstrated that large forces of soldiers, dragging mostly useless equipment, could rarely catch up with the hostile Indians; the army was far more likely to blunder into peaceful villages of Indians who were merely minding their own business.

Not much has been written about Indians who scouted for the army — and such scouts existed virtually from the time the first white man met the first Indian — but the fact is that if the army had not been able to employ Indian scouts, they would never have found *any* Indians. The Indian scouts were essential, not merely to help the army find Indians but to help the army find its own way as well. A few such scouts, because of their great knowledge of the country, acquired a certain fame. Black Beaver, a Delaware who scouted for Captain Randolph Marcy in Texas, was said to know every creek between the Columbia River gorge and the Rio Grande. In any pursuit situation the army would have been helpless without their Indian — or, often, half-breed — scouts. General Crook would never have found Geronimo in Mexico without Apache scouts to lead him, and the same is true of much Plains Indian warfare. Even *with* the scouts the army was rarely able to move fast enough to catch up with the hostiles they sought. When the whites did surprise a village, as Custer surprised Black Kettle on the Washita, it was usually because the Indians felt too secure in the knowledge that they were living peaceably to post adequate guards. If they weren't bothering the whites, they did not expect the whites to bother them. The lesson learned on the Bluewater in 1855 had to be learned over and over again: when white soldiers were in the mood to punish Indians, they would punish whatever group of Indians they came across, whether that particular group had committed hostilities or not.

Stephen Ambrose believes that it was Sherman who decided, after the miserable failure of the Hancock expedition, that he might as well give the peace policy a chance. Ambrose's contention is that Sherman, taking the long view, thought he saw a better way to eliminate the Indians than to keep sending out armies that couldn't find them. The better way would be to wait for the railroads. In a decade or less the hostiles of the northern plains would be caught between the Union Pacific and the Northern Pacific. Then the buffalo hunters — and, for that matter, the soldiers too — could ride at their ease right into the heart of Indian country and destroy the buffalo, the Indians' subsistence animal. This amounts to a leisurely — but sure — version of scorched earth, with E. H. Harriman and the other railroad magnates bearing much of the expense. The railroads would soon hurt the Indians far worse than the army had yet managed to. If this was indeed Sherman's thinking, then he was right. The buffalo lasted barely ten years after the railroads came.

9

The victory over Fetterman may have been sweet for the Indians, but the fort itself was still there, as were two others: Fort Reno and Fort C. F. Smith, all three in the heart of country that the Sioux felt was their own. Throughout the winter of 1866–67 the Indians kept a certain pressure on these forts, but, after Fetterman, the soldiers were cautious; about all the Sioux could do was make it difficult for them to gather firewood. To Red Cloud and the other Indian leaders the very presence of these forts was intolerable. In July of 1867, with Crazy Horse and a large force of warriors, Red Cloud attacked a kind of mini-fort that had been set up on the edge of the Bighorns, where wood could be cut in abundance. This little encampment, under the command of a Captain Powell, had only about forty men, but the wagons had been pulled into a tight circle and fortified with boxes stacked in and under them. The battle that ensued was thus called the Wagon Box Fight. The Indians picked off a few woodcutters, but the charge against the mini-fort failed. The soldiers were good marksmen, with plenty of ammunition. Had the Indians tried hitting the little troop from two sides at once, they might have overwhelmed them, but they didn't try that, and Captain Powell could not be induced to come out and play, as Fetterman had been. The Indians lost several warriors and the army regained a certain amount of face.

In the fall of 1867 General Sherman made a whirlwind tour of the prairies. He went up the Missouri and talked with Sitting Bull's people, parleyed with Spotted Tail in Nebraska, hurried south to Kansas, where he talked with the southern Cheyennes, the Arapahos, the Comanches, and the Kiowas, and then came back to Fort Laramie to talk, he hoped, with the Oglalas. Hurrying up and down the plains in pursuit of a general peace, Sherman preached farming, telling the Indians that it was finally time to give up the chase. The Indians were neither impressed nor persuaded. They hemmed and they hawed.

The peace commissioners, in approaching the Oglalas, caused a bit of awkwardness by asking for Red Cloud by name; in their eyes the struggle for the Powder River had become his war. To the Sioux and the

Cheyennes, it was not that simple. The "war" had consisted of a number of skirmishes and a few battles, some of which Red Cloud fought in and some of which he didn't. He was neither the first Indian nor the last to discover that popularity — or at least prominence — with the whites was apt to complicate relations back home.

To the Sioux and the Cheyennes the struggle for the Powder River was *their* war, not Red Cloud's, who at this point, though a respected war leader, was not a Big Belly or a man with any special moral authority. Their most respected man was still Old Man Afraid, and it was he who finally journeyed to Fort Laramie to talk with Sherman and the peace commissioners. Old Man Afraid agreed to nothing, but he did let the dignitaries know that peace was not likely until the forts along the Powder River were removed, a step the government was not willing to take — not yet. General Sherman, who had talked to Indians all the way from the Missouri to the Arkansas, went home well aware that he had made few converts to the farming life — nor would he while the buffalo still roamed.

In March of the next year, though, General Grant ordered the abandonment of

Fort C. F. Smith, Fort Reno, and Fort Phil Kearney. The battle for the Bozeman had become a stalemate. General Sherman was as convinced as ever that all the Indians would become, in time, what Chief Justice John Marshall had called them long before: domestic dependent nations. But Sherman also recognized that he could not immediately subdue these Indians by military means. The army's resources, whether of men or money, were not unlimited; the three little forts were soaking up money while producing nothing but aggravation.

The result of this decision was the famous treaty of 1868. It closed the forts and gave the Sioux and the Cheyennes forever the lands they had fought for so hard: the Dakotas west of the Missouri, the Black Hills, the land between the Platte and the Bighorn Mountains. No whites would be allowed to enter this territory, on penalty of arrest, a stern provision that was violated before the ink was dry on the paper. The Indians agreed to become, in white terms, "civilized" once the buffalo were gone. It is doubtful that many of the Sioux understood some of the more extreme clauses in regard to civilization, such as the provision for compulsory education.

Many dignitaries came to Fort Laramie

in August of 1868 for the signing of this treaty, and some Indians came, but Red Cloud didn't arrive. The whites who sat there, twiddling their thumbs — they included Sherman — got a good taste of Red Cloud's hauteur. In the end they left the papers and went home. Red Cloud, who had pursued some buffalo he ran into, finally showed up at the fort in November. The hated forts were by then gone, and the Sioux in full possession of their hunting grounds. The whites, for once, had backed down.

Meanwhile, to the south, in the same month that Red Cloud touched the pen, General Custer, in the famous dawn attack that was to provide a visual metaphor for so many movie westerns, wiped out Black Kettle on the Washita.

10

Crazy Horse had not gone to the peace conference at Fort Laramie in 1868. As usual, he avoided all conferences and continued to raid and hunt; now, free of the whites, he could again turn his attention to his traditional tribal enemies. He was a highly respected warrior, revered in the band for his willingness to share what he killed with the old and helpless; but he was not a chief, nor did he lead anyone other than his immediate companions, one of whom, his old friend Hump, was killed in a foolish raid on some Shoshones, a raid Crazy Horse had tried to discourage, mainly because it was rainy and slippery and the Shoshones were better mounted. (Black Elk said Crazy Horse never owned a good mount; no horse would carry him far, one theory being that the little stone pendant the medicine man Chips made for him was so heavy with magic that it broke the horses down.)

About three years after Red Cloud touched the pen at Fort Laramie, Crazy Horse, still unmarried, experienced a crisis that was marital rather than martial in nature. Though he was a Shirt-wearer, one who was supposed to provide an example of stable family behavior, his passion for Black Buffalo Woman had not abated. Ignoring the tribe's concern, he still hung around No Water's lodge, paying Black Buffalo Woman an unseemly amount of attention, even after she bore No Water a third child. No Water was not pleased with the state of things, but, like many husbands, he bore it.

Black Buffalo Woman, by Sioux custom, was not necessarily locked in for life with No Water. Any Sioux woman could divorce a husband who was no longer agreeable to her; all she had to do was place her husband's effects outside the lodge and she was divorced. But Black Buffalo Woman never quite worked up to this drastic step. She neither divorced No Water nor discouraged Crazy Horse, who might, within the terms of Sioux custom, have made No Water a formal offer for her. He could have offered his best horse, or several horses. Very likely No Water would have rejected this offer — from what we can tell at this distance he loved and valued his wife and had no intention of giving her up. But if Crazy Horse had made some sort of offer, at least the norms of civility that were expected of a Shirt-wearer would have been observed.

Crazy Horse, though, was indifferent to these formalities, or any formality. He always had been. What he did was wait until No Water had gone on a hunt, then he eloped with Black Buffalo Woman. The grand passion of his life could be denied no longer.

No Water was hardly the sort of husband to take this sort of behavior sitting down. When he returned from his hunt, he immediately borrowed a pistol from a warrior named Bad Heart Bull and went in pursuit of the lovers. This too was a violation of Sioux custom — Black Buffalo Woman had a right to go if she wanted to. But No Water went after her anyway.

The lovers enjoyed, at best, a very short idyll, perhaps only one night. They had not had time to go far before No Water found them, burst into the lodge where they were staying, and shot Crazy Horse just below his left nostril. Horrified, Black Buffalo Woman crawled out of the tent and skedaddled.

Versions of this violent incident differ. Some say Crazy Horse might have been able to grapple with No Water had not

Little Big Man grabbed his arm just as he was rising to meet the challenge. No Water said, "Friend, I have come!" or words to that effect; then he shot. If Little Big Man did grab Crazy Horse's arm, it of course foreshadows what he did in the fatal struggle at Fort Robinson six years later; it also fulfills Crazy Horse's dream, in which it was prophesied that he would only be injured if one of his own people held his arms to prevent him from fighting.

That is the poetic version, but there are other versions, none of which mention Little Big Man at all. He Dog, who was much exercised by this grave misbehavior, doesn't mention him. Since He Dog had to do much of the peacemaking, it would be odd that he doesn't mention Little Big Man if the latter had indeed been an actor in this old drama. He Dog says the lovers had been in the lodge of Little Shield when No Water caught up with them.

In any case, quite a mess had been made. No Water was brother to the prominent Sioux twins Black Twin and White Twin, of the Bad Faces, Red Cloud's village. No Water went to his brother Black Twin, who made a sweat lodge, purified No Water of what he supposed was a murder, and prepared to fight Crazy Horse's people, if necessary.

Fortunately for all concerned, Crazy Horse wasn't dead. The bullet broke his jaw, but after a day or two it was clear that he would live. Still, feelings ran high in both camps. The peacemakers had to work skillfully and quickly to prevent what could have become a bloody feud. Black Buffalo Woman, like many a wife taken in adultery, fled, but was eventually persuaded to return to her husband. Crazy Horse made it a condition that she not be punished, and she wasn't. No Water gave Crazy Horse his best horse as a peace offering, but the two never really made it up. No Water and Black Buffalo Woman went to live with Red Cloud's band. Once Crazy Horse encountered No Water while on a hunt and chased him all the way across the Yellowstone River before allowing him to escape.

He Dog, remembering this sorry sequence of events sixty years later, was still indignant at the thought of the damage it had done to tribal harmony. No Water blamed the medicine man Chips, saying Chips had made Black Buffalo Woman a potion that had caused her to lose her reason; but among the elders of the band, Crazy Horse was judged to be the most at fault. He had taken another man's wife and had done it with complete disregard for custom and propriety, thus seriously threatening tribal unity. Much diplomacy had to be practiced to prevent war between one band and the other. No Water, in particular, never forgot. He was an eager member of the party that went to the Spotted Tail agency to arrest Crazy Horse at the end.

Crazy Horse could not, after this, be a Shirt-wearer. He had failed in the Shirt-wearer's first duty, which was to put the interest of the tribe first. When Elinor Hinman asked He Dog all those years later who had been made a Shirt-wearer in Crazy Horse's place, He Dog replied that nobody had. The institution itself fell into disuse after this foolishness, which left such a bad taste in people's mouths that the whole thing lapsed.

Black Buffalo Woman's fourth child, a daughter, was notably light-skinned; perhaps the child of Crazy Horse, she lived into the 1940s.

Not long after this the tribe saw to it that Crazy Horse took a wife, an agreeable woman named Black Shawl, whom he accepted and, it would seem, came to love. Rather like Yeats, who after his failure with Maud Gonne came to be happy with his kind wife George, Crazy Horse seems to have achieved domestic content with Black Shawl, who, unfortunately, was afflicted with tuberculosis. One of the reasons Crazy Horse developed a friendship with Dr. Valentine McGillycuddy was that the doctor was so steadfast in his efforts to cure Black Shawl.

Later, Crazy Horse took a second wife, a half-Cheyenne, half-French girl named Nellie Larrabee (sometimes spelled Laverie); there is a picture of her in Ian Frazier's *Great Plains*. Very probably he never quite got over Black Buffalo Woman, about whose later life nothing is known.

Thus the great passion of Crazy Horse's life failed and brought serious disorder to his people. It was not long after this that he also suffered the loss of his reckless brother Little Hawk, who was killed when he foolishly attacked some well-armed miners.

Meanwhile, though the Sioux had their treaty, the railroads were coming and with them the whites. There was no serious attempt made to police the area that was then, by law, off-limits to the whites. Who was supposed to have policed an area that vast, anyway? By 1872 the railroads had come so far that Custer, Sheridan, Buffalo Bill Cody, and other dignitaries could take

Grand Duke Alexis of Russia on a buffalo hunt, with the grand duke traveling well into Kansas in the comfort of his railroad car.

To the north, things were still quiet. The Northern Pacific was only just edging into North Dakota. It would be a while before it threatened the Sioux sanctuary.

But no quiet, no peace, really lasted long; the endgame was now about to begin. In late summer of 1872 a force of several hundred soldiers pushed up the Yellowstone River into eastern Montana, precipitating the first major conflict between the wild, mainly undisturbed northern Sioux, including Sitting Bull's people, the Hunkpapas.

Crazy Horse had perhaps drifted north by then; he may have been dissatisfied with the more and more passive conditions to the south, where both Red Cloud and Spotted Tail were now firmly (and permanently) committed to peace. Both had been given agencies of their own; they made no more war on the whites. Spotted Tail was criticized in some quarters for being, in a manner of speaking, a kind of Vichy Indian — but this is quite unfair. Spotted Tail was never a toady, and never sycophantic in his dealings with the whites.

Given a choice, probably he would have been happy just to get out of the way; but the Brulés, whom he led, really couldn't get out of the way. So Spotted Tail negotiated, for the most part effectively. He survived his two-year imprisonment with his dignity intact, and it was to remain intact until the end, when, like Sitting Bull, he was killed by one of his own people, a rival named Crow Dog.

But agency life, with its endless compromising and its constant haggling with the white agents, would never have appealed to Crazy Horse, any more than it appealed to Sitting Bull.

The engagement that Sitting Bull and Crazy Horse fought in August of 1872 came near to being a disaster for the Indians. The force against them, some four hundred soldiers, was well armed and could not be tempted into any rashness. Crazy Horse had learned at the Wagon Box Fight how ineffective bows and arrows were against soldiers who were both well armed and competently led. In this fight in the north the Sioux were very daring, but simply could not get close enough to the soldiers to inflict any damage without paying a huge price in lives. As it was, several of the unrestrainable young Sioux were killed early on. It was in this fight that Sitting Bull astonished everyone, Sioux and soldier alike: he sat down in a meadow, in range of the riflemen, casually filled a pipe, lit it, and smoked it, while bullets cut the grass all around him. Crazy Horse, perhaps jealous of Sitting Bull's sangfroid, reportedly made a reckless dash right across the soldiers' front, and had his horse shot out from under him for his trouble, after which the Sioux called off the battle.

Throughout the later stages of these conflicts on the plains, up to and including the Custer battle, the Sioux were at a disadvantage because they were so poorly armed. Only a small percentage had guns, and they were usually poor guns at that; even the Sioux who had reliable firearms seldom had much ammunition. They could never afford to match the white men gun for gun and bullet for bullet. From the first the white authorities had been far-sighted enough to deny the Indians guns. Even the bravest warrior, armed with a bow and arrow, could only do so much when up against a well-prepared soldier with a gun.

Though the financial panic of 1873 slowed the progress of the Northern Pacific somewhat, its surveyors were nonetheless pushing relentlessly west, well protected by a force that in the popular mind was commanded by George Armstrong Custer. In fact the commander was a modest officer named Stanley. It was while this large force proceeded along the Yellowstone, obviously now in what was supposed to be Sioux country, that Crazy Horse encountered Custer for the first time. The Sioux and the Cheyennes caught Custer and his small detachment napping — literally, in the case of Custer himself — but the Sioux initially intended no big fight. They tried to run off the army's horse herd, and when that plan was thwarted, tried a decoy maneuver similar to the one that had worked with Fetterman. Custer didn't go for it; but then the Cheyennes noticed Custer's hair, which was still long, and remembered the massacre on the Washita — perhaps a few of the warriors who had survived that fight were now back visiting their northern cousins. The Cheyennes attacked, but Custer drove them off. Custer then turned back, and the Indians disengaged. There was little loss of life. Custer thought Sitting Bull was the leader in this skirmish; what he knew of Crazy Horse, if anything, is unclear. Crazy Horse had never been to a meeting with the whites. He had a big reputation with his own people but had as yet received no mention in the popular press. Back east the severe financial panic had for a time driven mere Indian fights off the front pages anyway: the gilding was suddenly beginning to flake off the Gilded Age; all was confusion, dismay, frustration. There no longer seemed to be enough money; specifically, not enough gold. The conservatives were happy to have the country on a gold standard, as long as there was enough gold for the economy to expand; but in the summer of 1873, there wasn't enough. Paper money had not yet fully caught on.

Fortunately for the nation, unfortunately for the Sioux, the Black Hills awaited; there had long been rumors of large gold deposits in the Sioux's holy hills. Awkwardly, though, for the leaders of the whites, there was the binding and much-publicized treaty of 1868, unequivocally giving those very hills to the Sioux forever, with unusually clear provisions that they, the whites, were to be kept out. The U.S. government had broken many treaties with the Indians; some would say they had broken *all* of them — the writer Alex Shoumatoff recently reckoned the total at 378 — but few of these breakages involved so much squirming and soul searching and public posturing as the treaty of 1868. General Sheridan began to mutter unconvincingly about treaty violations on the part of the Sioux, but in fact the Sioux were behaving nicely at the time, as the same general had admitted in another context. There were no grounds for breaching the treaty of 1868 except the grounds the whites finally always used: The United States *wanted* the Black Hills and all the gold that might be there. A big first step toward the taking of them was the expedition that brought General Custer back to the west and produced the famous photograph of a seemingly endless line of wagons proceeding through a valley in the Black Hills. This expedition soon fulfilled its main, though unstated, purpose, which was to find gold in sufficient quantities to quench the thirst of the starving markets.

In Custer's excited imagination the gold his geologists located at French Creek was so abundant and so easy to get that he could kick it up with the toe of his boot. In reality it was not quite that easy to get, but the gold *was* there, and, as time has proven, there in quantity. The trail Custer blazed into the Black Hills on that occasion became known to the Indians by a name he despised: the Sioux called it the Thieves' Road.

Many of Custer's scouts refused to go into the hills with him, fearing the Sioux, but he went anyway; as soon as traces of gold were detected, he sent the famous white scout Lonesome Charley Reynolds through dangerous country to Fort Laramie to announce this great find to the world. Lonesome Charley made it through and sent the telegram. In August, Custer emerged and described the beauties of the Black Hills in mouthwatering terms. In another life he would have made a wonderful real-estate developer. In this case he sold one of the most beautiful pieces of real estate in the west to a broke, depressed public who couldn't wait to get into those hills and start scratching up gold.

The Sioux did not oppose this expedition; Custer saw few Indians on his trip. Sitting Bull and his Hunkpapas were to the north and west; and Crazy Horse, about this time, was grieving for his little daughter They-Are-Afraid-of-Her, who had died, probably of cholera. When he returned to his camp and found that she had died, he located her burial scaffold and stayed with her several days. He did not get to raise the light-skinned daughter of Black Buffalo Woman, and his parentage of that child is conjectural anyway. But They-Are-Afraid-of-Her was his child, and he loved her deeply. Her loss took some of the fight out of him, for a while.

Again, though, I would enter the caveat that for much of his life only Crazy Horse's immediate companions knew where he was or what he did. In the early 1870s personal losses began to pile up: Hump, Lone Bear, Little Hawk, They-Are-Afraid-of-Her. Many commentators, Erik Erikson among them, have spoken of the Sioux's profound devotion to their children — the loss of this child would have been a terribly severe blow.

The historians who have concerned themselves most closely with Crazy Horse perhaps naturally slip into a Crazy Horse–centric view of Plains Indian life; they put too much weight on the memories of a few old Sioux and begin to believe that if there was a battle that Crazy Horse *might* have been in, he *was* in it. In a curious way the historians' approaches to Red Cloud and Crazy Horse are opposite: they tend to take Red Cloud *out* of battles he may well have been in and put Crazy Horse *in* battles he may well have missed. Of course it is true that Crazy Horse got noticed in most of the battles he fought in because of his extreme daring. He would usually have been the Indian the soldiers shot at first. How much of a tactical sense he developed from all this fighting is not easy to know. Since fighting was a big part of his life, we may safely assume that he observed and learned; how much of what he learned was merely common sense we don't know. He Dog says Crazy Horse was the only Indian he knew who always dismounted to shoot, which certainly shows good sense; and he did not want to fight the Shoshones the day Hump was killed for the excellent commonsense reasons that the ground was slippery and the Shoshones had better horses.

The fight with Crook on the Rosebud, which we will come to later, was on a different scale. Perhaps this was a strategically thought-out attack on the part of the Sioux Indians; or it may have been only an unusually persistent attack, because, for various reasons, the Sioux were particularly confident that day and had caught Three Stars Crook on disadvantageous terrain. For once they may simply have felt they had the numbers to do the job. But to pretend that we can follow Crazy Horse's thinking at the Rosebud is hubris, in the main. In a great many shadowy cases where Crazy Horse fought, or may have fought, the data is simply not firm; in making him a master strategist — as opposed to merely a very daring warrior — the historian walks on very thin ice indeed.

11

By the summer of 1875 the crisis over the Black Hills could no longer be postponed. Custer's grand announcement caught the nation's attention: after that the miners could not be held back. The government was obviously going to find a way to take back the Black Hills; but just as obviously, they were not going to be able to do so without difficulty and without criticism. The whites in the peace party were vocal; they and others of various parties thought the government ought to at least *try* to honor its agreements, particularly those made as solemnly and as publicly as this one. So there ensued a period of wiggling and squirming, on both the part of the government and the part of the Sioux, many of whom had become agency Indians by this time. The free life of the hunting Sioux was still just possible, but only in certain areas: the Powder River, parts of Montana, and the Dakotas, where the buffalo still existed in some numbers.

By this time most of the major Indian

leaders had made a realistic assessment of the situation and drawn the obvious conclusion, which was that their old way of life was rapidly coming to an end. One way or another they were going to have to walk the white man's road — or else fight until they were all killed. Crazy Horse and Sitting Bull were among the most determined of the hostiles; Red Cloud and Spotted Tail, rivals at this point, both had settled constituencies. They were administrators essentially, struggling to get more food and better goods out of their respective agents. As more and more Indians came in and enrollment lists swelled, this became a full-time job, and a vexing and frustrating one at that.

There were of course many Indians who tried to walk a middle road, unwilling to completely give up the old ways but recognizing that the presence of whites in what had once been their country was now a fact of life. Young Man Afraid, son of the revered Old Man Afraid, was one of the middle-of-the-roaders.

The whites at first tried pomp and circumstance, bringing the usual suspects yet again to Washington, hoping to tempt them — Red Cloud, Spotted Tail, anyone — to sell the Black Hills. They would have liked to have Sitting Bull and Crazy Horse at this grand parley, or even a moderate such as Young Man Afraid, but none of these men nor any of the principal hostiles wanted anything to do with this mini-summit. Red Cloud and Spotted Tail had no authority to sell the Black Hills, or to do anything about them at all, a fact the white authorities should have realized by this time. There were still thousands of Sioux on the northern plains who had not given their consent to anything. The mini-summit fizzled.

Red Cloud and Spotted Tail had probably long since concluded that the whites were going to take the Black Hills: When had they not taken land they wanted? The two leaders, for a time, probably hoped to get the best obtainable price rather than see their land taken for nothing, which is what eventually happened. But most Sioux had not achieved this level of realism, or cynicism, yet. They thought the Black Hills were theirs forever.

Parade diplomacy having failed in Washington, the government decided to take its roadshow west. In the early fall of 1875 they staged a big conclave at a place carefully chosen to be midway between Red Cloud's agency and Spotted Tail's — they knew they couldn't afford to further inflame that rivalry. Historians who argue that either the Fort Laramie council of 1851 or the massing at the Little Bighorn was the greatest gathering of Plains Indians ever tend to forget the Black Hills council of 1875, which was at least a challenger. I don't think anyone can present an accurate count of how many Indians came, or at least hovered in the vicinity, but all agree there were a lot. The Blackfeet came, and the Cheyennes, and at least seven or eight of the major bands of the Sioux. Sitting Bull held aloof, as did Crazy Horse, meaning that both the Hunkpapas and the Oglalas were without their most resolute resisters. Just as Red Cloud was getting ready to deliver one of his lengthy orations, a very great many warriors, by one reckoning seven thousand (here again I can't imagine who was counting), rode out of the hills and circled the council tent. Then Little Big Man made his dramatic charge right up to the feet of the peace commissioners, threatening to shoot anyone who wanted to sell the Black Hills. Whether Little Big Man was really speaking for Crazy Horse is hard to say, but all witnesses agree that his entrance made for a touchy situation. The warriors were very stirred up; there was danger, for a time, of serious violence.

Fortunately, Young Man Afraid — he was by this time an Indian policeman — stepped forward and managed to quiet the situation. Thanks both to his valor and to his irreproachable character, he enjoyed an authority almost equal to his father's; the warriors, much to the peace commissioner's relief, would not go against him. The hostiles soon mostly left and the seasoned bargainers got down to business. Various sums were bruited about, but in the end nobody agreed to anything, though soon afterward, miners poured into the Black Hills so rapidly that the land that was to have been the Sioux's forever had more whites on it than Indians; the same thing happened in Oklahoma, where the citizens of the Five Civilized Tribes were soon outnumbered three to one on their own land.

The best the government could do at this time was to establish, by fiat, a reservation system and to criminalize the Indians who didn't feel like parking themselves within the boundaries of whichever reservation they were assigned to. In the fall of 1871, Grant ordered them to hurry on in and get themselves enrolled by January, ignoring the fact that few Indians cared to move their camps in the wintertime.

No officer in the field — and this now included the redoubtable George Crook, Three Stars to the Indians — supposed that the nonagency Sioux would simply hurry in and sign up. Crazy Horse, who was then riding with Black Twin (No Water's brother), sent back word that it was a particularly inconvenient time to move; perhaps he would look more favorably on the proposal in the spring. The hostile Sioux didn't take Grant's order seriously, and neither did the military men who marched off, confidently for the most part, to whip them into submission. The Indians stayed wherever they happened to be, and the army got on the move, though in fact it didn't fight much that winter of 1875–76. It proved no more convenient for General Crook to march on Crazy Horse than it would have for Crazy Horse to come in.

Many Indians by this time had taken to wintering in the agencies and then drifting off again once the weather improved. Thousands came in, but when spring came, many of them went out again.

Crazy Horse, meanwhile, was enjoying what was to be his last more or less unharassed winter as a free Indian. How well or how clearly he realized that his time was ending, we don't know. Perhaps he still thought that if the people fought fiercely and didn't relent they could beat back the whites, not all the way to the Platte perhaps, but at least out of the Powder River country. We don't really know what he was thinking and should be cautious about making him more geopolitically attuned than he may have been. At this juncture nobody had really agreed to anything, but as the spring of 1876 approached, the army directed a number of its major players toward the northern plains. To the south, on the plains of Texas, the so-called Red River War was over. The holdouts among the Comanches and the Kiowas had been defeated and their horse herd destroyed. Ranald Mackenzie and Nelson A. Miles both distinguished themselves in the Red River War and were soon sent north to help subdue the Cheyennes and the northern Sioux. General Crook was already in the field, and Gibbon, Terry, and, of course, Custer were soon on their way.

By March of 1876 a great many Indians were moving north, toward Sitting Bull and the Hunkpapas, ready for a big hunt and possibly for a big fight with the whites, if the whites insisted on it, as in fact they did. The Little Bighorn in eastern Montana was the place chosen for this great gathering of native peoples, which swelled with more and more Indians as warmer weather came.

General Crook — Three Stars, or the Grey Fox — struck first. He located what the scout Frank Grouard assured him was Crazy Horse's village, made a dawn attack, captured the village, destroyed the ample provender it contained (some of which his own hungry men could happily have eaten), but killed few Indians. Where Crazy Horse actually was at this time is a matter much debated, but the camp Crook destroyed seems not to have been his. It may have been He Dog's, who was apparently on his way to the Red Cloud agency, hoping to avoid trouble. For Crook the encounter was more vexation than triumph. The Sioux regrouped that night and got back most of their horses, and the fight drove these peace-seeking Indians back north toward Sitting Bull. Crook continued to suppose that he had destroyed Crazy Horse's village; no doubt some of his friends were there, but the man himself was elsewhere.

12

A vast amount has been written about the great gathering of Indians who assembled in Montana in the early summer of 1876. It was to be the last mighty grouping of native peoples on the Great Plains of America. For the older people it evoked memories of summer gatherings before — reunions of a sort — such as had once been held at Bear Butte, near Crazy Horse's birthplace. Many of these Indians probably knew that what was occurring was in the nature of a last fling: there might be no opportunity for such a grand occasion again. Most of the Indians who gathered knew that the soldiers were coming, but they didn't care: their numbers were so great that they considered themselves invincible. Many Indians, from many tribes, remembered it as a last great meeting and mingling, a last good time. Historically, from this point on, there is a swelling body of reminiscence about the events of the spring and summer of 1876. Indeed, from the time the armies went into the field in 1876 to the end of the conflict there is a voluminous memoir literature to be sifted through — most of it military memoirs written by whites. Much of this found its way into the small-town newspapers that by then dotted the plains. These memoirs are still emerging. In 1996 four letters written by the wife of a captain who was at Fort Robinson when Crazy Horse was killed were discovered and published. The woman's name was Angie Johnson. It had taken more than a century for this literature to trickle out of the attics and scrapbooks of America, and it is still trickling. Of course it didn't take that long for the stately memoirs of Sheridan and Sherman and Miles and the rest to be published.

Though the bulk of this memoir literature is by white soldiers, quite a few of the Sioux and the Cheyennes who fought at the Little Bighorn managed to get themselves interviewed here and there. It is part of the wonder of *Son of the Morning Star* that Evan S. Connell Jr. has patiently located many of these obscurely published reminiscences from both sides of the fight and placed them in his narrative in such a way as to create a kind of mosaic of firsthand comment. These memoirs don't answer all the questions, or even very many of them, but it is still nice to know what the participants *thought* happened, even if what we're left with is a kind of mesquite thicket of opinion, dense with guessing, theory, and speculation. Any great military conflict — Waterloo, Gettysburg, etc. — leaves behind a similar confusion, a museum of memories but an extremely untidy one. Did the general say that or do this? Was Gall behind Custer or in front of him or nowhere near him? The mind that is troubled by unanswered and perhaps unanswerable questions should perhaps avoid military history entirely. Battles are messy things. Military historians have often to resort to such locutions as "it would at this juncture probably be safe to assume. . . ." Stephen Ambrose is precisely right (and uncommonly frank) when he says plainly that much of the fun of studying the Battle of the Little Bighorn is the free rein it offers to the imagination. Once pointed toward this battle, the historical imagination tends to bolt, like the uncheckable horse that carried poor Lieutenant Collins to his death near the Platte Bridge. Certainly the field of battle that the Indians called the Greasy Grass has caused many imaginations to bolt.

13

What we know for sure is that when June rolled around in 1876 there were a great many Indians, of several tribes, camped in southern Montana, with a fair number of soldiers moving west and north to fight them. Early June of that year may have been a last moment of confidence for the Plains Indians: they were many, they had meat, and they were in *their* place: let the soldiers come.

This buildup of confidence was capped by what was probably the best-reported dream vision in native American history — namely, Sitting Bull's vision of soldiers falling upside down into camp. This important vision did not come to the great Hunkpapa spontaneously; instead, it was elaborately prepared for. Sitting Bull allowed a friend to cut one hundred small pieces of flesh from his arms, after which he danced, staring at the sun until he fainted. When he came out of his swoon he heard a voice and had a vision of soldiers as numerous as grasshoppers falling upside down into camp. There were some who were skeptical of Sitting Bull — he could be a difficult sort — but this vision, coming as it did at the end of a great sundance, convinced most of his people that if the soldiers did come they would fall. (It is worth mentioning that Sitting Bull had mixed luck with visions: not long before his death a meadowlark, speaking in Sioux, told him that his own people would kill him — which is what occurred.)

Shortly after this great vision of soldiers falling had been reported and considered, some Cheyenne scouts arrived with the news that the great General Crook was coming from the south with a lot of soldiers and also a considerable body of Crow and Shoshone scouts. This was a sign that Sitting Bull had not danced in vain, although Crook never got very close to the great encampment, because Crazy Horse, Sitting Bull, and a large force immediately went south to challenge him on the Rosebud, where the first of the two famous battles fought that summer was joined.

When the Indians attacked, Crook's thousand-man force was very strung out, with soldiers on both sides of the river, in terrain that was broken and difficult. Crow scouts were the first to spot the great party from the north; by common agreement the Crows and Shoshones fought their hearts out that day, probably saving Crook from the embarrassment of an absolute rout. But Crazy Horse, Black Twin, Bad Heart Bull, and many others were just as determined. Once or twice Crook almost succeeded in forming an effective battle line, but Crazy Horse and the others kept dashing right into it, fragmenting Crook's force and preventing a serious counterattack. There was much close-quarter, hand-to-hand fighting. In a rare anticipation of women-in-combat, a Cheyenne woman rushed in at some point and saved her brother, who was surrounded. (The Cheyennes afterward referred to the Battle of the Rosebud as the Battle Where the Girl Saved Her Brother.) Crook struggled all day, trying to mount a strong offensive, but the attackers were so persistent that they thwarted him. Finally the day waned and shadows began to fall across the Rosebud. The Indians, having enjoyed a glorious day of battle, went home. They had turned Three Stars back, allowing him nowhere near the great gathering on the Little Bighorn.

Because the Indians left the field when the day was over, Crook claimed a victory, but nobody believed him, including (probably) himself. The Battle of the Rosebud was one of his most frustrating memories. It was indeed a remarkable battle between forces almost equally matched; in some ways it was more interesting than the fight at the Little Bighorn eight days later. Neither side could mount a fully decisive offensive, and both sides suffered unusually high casualities but kept fighting. The whites had no choice, of course; their adversaries in this case fought with extreme determination. The body count for the two sides varies with the commentator: George Hyde puts Crook's loss as high as fifty-seven men, a number that presumably includes many Crows and Shoshones who fell that day; Stephen Ambrose says it was twenty-eight men; Stanley Vestal says it was ten; and Robert Utley and Evan S. Connell Jr. claim it was nine. The attacking Sioux and Cheyennes may themselves have lost over thirty men, an enormous casualty rate for a native force. Accustomed as we are to the wholesale slaughter of the two world wars, or even of the Civil War, it is hard to keep in mind that when Indian fought Indian a death count of more than three or four was unusual.

At the end of the day General Crook at

last accepted the advice his scouts had offered him earlier, which was that there were too many Indians up ahead for him to fight.

Had the full extent of Crook's difficulties on the Rosebud been known to the forces moving west into Montana, the sensible officers — that is, Gibbon and Terry — would have then proceeded with extreme caution; but it is unlikely that any trouble of Crook's would have slowed Custer one whit. Even if he had known that the Indians had sent Crook packing, it is hard to imagine that he would have proceeded differently. He had plenty of explicit — and, at the last, desperate — warnings from his own scouts, but he brushed these aside as he hurried the 7th Cavalry on to its doom. He plainly did not want to give his pessimistic scouts the time of day. He wanted to whip the Indians and, besides that, he wanted to do it by himself, with just the 7th Cavalry. He refused the offer of extra troops and also refused a Gatling gun, for fear that it might slow him down and allow the Indians to get away. It was only in the last minutes of his life that Custer finally realized that the Indians were fighting, not running. Custer was as convinced as Fetterman that he could whip whatever body of Indians he could persuade to face him. He meant to win, he meant to win alone, and he meant to win rapidly, before any other officers arrived to dilute his glory.

14

This book is about Crazy Horse, not Custer. That erratic egotist has been studied more than enough; he has even been the subject of one of the best books written about the west, Evan S. Connell Jr.'s *Son of the Morning Star*. Historians have speculated endlessly about why he did what he did at the Little Bighorn, on the twenty-fifth of June, 1876; and yet what he did was perfectly in keeping with his nature. He did what he had always done: push ahead, disregard orders, start a fight, win it unassisted if possible, then start another fight. He had seldom done otherwise, and there was no reason at all to expect him to do otherwise in Montana.

It may be true, as several writers have suggested, that he was covertly running for president that summer. The Democratic convention was just convening: a flashy victory and a timely telegram might have put him in contention for the nomination. Maybe, as Connell suggests, he thought he could mop up on the Sioux, race down to the Yellowstone, hop on the steamer *Far West*, and make it to the big Centennial parade on July fourth. So he marched his men most of the night and flung them into battle when — as a number of Indians noted — they were so tired their legs shook when they dismounted. As usual, he did only minimal reconnaissance, and convinced himself on no evidence whatever that the Indians must be running away from him, not toward him. The highly experienced scouts who were with him — the half-breed Mitch Bouyer and the Crows Bloody Knife and Half Yellow Face — all told Custer that they would die if they descended into the valley where the Indians were. None of them, in all their many years on the plains, had ever seen anything to match this great encampment. All the scouts knew that the valley ahead was for them the valley of death. Half Yellow Face, poetically, told Custer that they would all go home that day by a road they did not know. The fatalism of these scouts is a story in itself. Mitch Bouyer, who knew exactly what was coming, sent the young scout Curly away, but then himself rode on with Custer, to his death.

Whatever they said, what wisdom they offered, Custer ignored. It may be that he *was* running for president, but it is hard to believe that he would have done anything differently even if it had been an off year politically. Reno and Benteen, whom he had forced to split off, both testified much later that they didn't believe Custer had any plan when he pressed his attack. He was — and long had been — the most aggressive general in the American army. It didn't matter to him how many Indians there were. When he saw an enemy, he attacked, and would likely have done so even if he had no political prospects.

In the week between the fight on the Rosebud and the one at the Little Bighorn, Crazy Horse went back to the big party. The great General Crook had been whipped — the Indians felt invincible again, though some commentators have suggested that a sense of doom and foreboding hung over the northern plains during this fatal week: Indian and soldier alike were said to have felt it. Something dark and terrible was about to happen — and yet it was high summer in one of the most beautiful places in Montana, the one time when that vast plain is usually free of rain clouds or snow clouds. But this summer, Death was coming to a feast, and many felt his approach. On the morning of the battle, when most of the Sioux and Cheyennes were happily and securely going about their domestic business, never supposing that any soldiers would be foolish enough to attack them, Crazy Horse, it is said, marked, in red pigment, a Bloody Hand on both of his horse's hips, and drew an arrow and a bloody red hand on both sides of his horse's neck. Oglala scouts had been keeping watch on Custer, following his movements closely. Crazy Horse either knew or sensed that the fatal day had come.

15

The Battle of the Little Bighorn, June 25 and 26, 1876, is one of the most famous battles in world history. I doubt that any other American battle — not the Alamo, not Gettysburg — has spawned a more extensive or more diverse literature. There are books, journals, newsletters, one or another of which has by now printed every scrap of reminiscence that has been dredged up. Historians of both the professional and the amateur persuasions have poured forth voluminous speculations, wondering what would have happened if somebody — usually the unfortunate Major Reno — had done something differently, or if Custer hadn't foolishly split his command, or if and if and if. Though the battle took place more than one hundred and twenty years ago, debate has not much slackened. In fact, the sudden rise in Native American studies has resulted in increased reprinting of Indian as opposed to white reminiscences; now the Sioux and the Cheyennes are pressing the debate.

A number of white historians have argued that one or another Indian leader made the decisive moves that doomed Custer and the 7th; for these historians the battle was decided by strategy and generalship, not numbers. Both Stephen Ambrose and Mari Sandoz have written many pages about the brilliance of Crazy Horse in flanking Custer and seizing the high ground — today called Custer Hill — thus ending Custer's last hope of establishing a defensive position that might have held until reinforcements arrived. Others argue for their favorite chief, whether Gall, Two Moon, or another. Evan Connell, in his lengthy account of the battle, scarcely mentions Crazy Horse's part in it. All these arguments, of course, depend on Indian memory, plus study of the battleground itself. To me they seem to be permanently ambiguous, potent rather than conclusive. It is indeed an area of study where historians can give free rein to their imaginations; what Stephen Ambrose doesn't mention is that the Sioux and the Cheyennes, in remembering this battle, might be giving *their* imaginations a little running room as well. A world in which all whites are poets and all Indians sober reporters is not the world as most of us know it.

We are likely never to know for sure who killed Custer. He had cut his famous hair short for this campaign; had it still been long, many Indians might have recognized him. It is as well to keep in mind that as many as two thousand horses may have been in motion during this battle; between the dust they raised and the gunsmoke the scene would soon have become phantasmagorical; it would have been difficult for anyone to see well, or far. It is thus little wonder that no one recognized Custer. At some sharp moment Custer must have realized that his reasoning had been flawed. The Indians he had assumed were running away were actually coming to kill him, and there were a lot of them. Whether he much regretted his error is doubtful. Fighting was what Custer did, battle thrilled him, and now he was right in the dead thick of the biggest Indian fight of all. He may have enjoyed himself right up to the moment he fell.

For his men, of course, it was a different story. They had been marching since the middle of the night; a lot of them were so tired they could barely lift their guns. For them it was dust, weariness, terror, and death.

No one knows for sure how many Indians fought in this battle, but two thousand is a fair estimate, give or take a few hundred. Besides their overpowering numbers they were also highly psyched by the great sundance and their recent victory over Crook. When Major Reno and his men appeared at the south end of the great four-mile village, the Indians were primed. Reno might have charged them and produced, at least, disarray, but he didn't; the Indians soon chased him back across the Little Bighorn and up a bluff, where he survived, just barely. A lucky shot hit Bloody Knife, the Crow scout, square in the head; Major Reno, standing near, was splattered with his brain matter — some think this gory accident undid Major Reno, but we will never know the state of his undoneness, if any. Gall, the Hunk-papa warrior who, by common agreement, was a major factor in this battle, soon had fifteen hundred warriors mounted and ready to fight. If Major Reno *had* charged the south end of the village, he might have been massacred as thoroughly as Custer.

Exactly when Crazy Horse entered the battle is a matter of debate. Some say he rode out and skirmished a little with Reno's men; others believe he was still in his lodge when Reno arrived and that he was only interested in the larger fight with Custer. Most students of the battle think that when it dawned on Custer that he was in a fight for survival, not glory, he turned north, toward the high ground, hoping to establish a defensive redoubt on the hill, or rise, that is now named for him. But Crazy Horse, perhaps at the head of as many as a thousand warriors himself, flanked him and seized that high ground, sealing Custer's doom while, incidentally, making an excellent movie role for Errol Flynn and a number of other leading men.

So Crazy Horse may have done, but it was Gall and *his* thousand or so warriors who turned back Reno and then harried Custer so hard that the 7th Cavalry — the soldiers who fell into camp, as in Sitting Bull's vision — could never really establish *any* position. If Crazy Horse did flank Custer, it was of course good quarterbacking, but it hardly seems possible now to insist that any one move was decisive. Gall and his men might have finished Custer without much help from anyone — Gall had lost his wife and daughter early in the battle and was fighting out his anger and his grief.

From this distance of years the historians can argue until their teeth rot that one man or another was decisive in this battle, but all these arguments are unprovable now. What's certain is that George Armstrong Custer was very foolish, a glory hound who ignored orders, skipped or disregarded his reconnaissance, and charged, all but blindly, into a situation in which, whatever the quality of Indian generalship, he was quickly overwhelmed by numbers.

What I think of when I walk that battleground is dust. Once or twice in my life I rode out with as many as thirty cowboys — I remember the dust that small, unhurried group made. The dust of two thousand milling, charging horses would have been something else altogether; the battleground would soon have been a hell of dust, smoke, shooting, hacking; once the two groups of fighting men closed with one another, visibility could not have been good. Custer received a wound in the breast and one in the temple, either of which would have been fatal. His corpse was neither scalped nor mutilated. Bad Soup, a Hunkpapa, is said to have pointed out Custer's corpse to White Bull. "There he lies," he said. "He thought he was going to be the greatest man in the world. But there he is."

Most of the poetic remarks that come to us from this battle are the work of writers who interviewed Indians, or those who knew Indians, who thought they remembered Bad Soup saying something, or Half Yellow Face making (probably in sign) the remark about the road we do not know, or Bloody Knife staring long at the sun that morning, knowing that he would not be alive to see it go down behind the hills that evening. All we can conclude now is that Bloody Knife and Bad Soup and Half Yellow Face were right, even if they didn't say the words that have been attributed to them.

Hundreds of commentators, from survivors who fought in the battle to historians who would not be born until long years after the dust had settled in the valley of the Little Bighorn, have developed opinions about scores of issues which remain, in the end, completely opaque. Possibly Crazy Horse fought as brilliantly as some think — we will never really know. But he and Sitting Bull and Two Moon survived the battle and Custer didn't. General Grant, no sentimentalist, put the blame for the defeat squarely on Custer, and said so bluntly. The Indians made no serious attempt to root out and destroy Reno, though they could have. Victory over Long Hair was enough; Black Kettle was well revenged.

The next day, to Major Reno's vast relief, the great gathering broke up, the Indians melting away into the sheltering vastness of the plains.

16

What did the Sioux and Cheyenne leaders think at this point? What did they feel? Several commentators have suggested that once the jubilation of victory subsided, a mood of foreboding returned. Perhaps the tribes recognized that they were likely never to be so unified again — and they were not. Probably the leaders knew that they were likely never to have such a one-sided military victory again, either — a victory that was thrown them because of the vaingloriousness of one white officer.

Or perhaps they didn't think in these terms at all — not yet. With the great rally over, the great battle won, they broke up and got on with their hunting. Perhaps a few did reckon that something was over now, but it is doubtful that many experienced the sense of climax and decline as poetically as Old Lodge Skins in Thomas Berger's *Little Big Man*: "Yes, my son," he says,

it is finished now, because what more can you do to an enemy than beat him?

Were we fighting red man against red man — the way we used to, because that is a man's profession, and besides it is enjoyable — it would now be the turn of the other side to whip us. We would fight as hard as ever and perhaps would win again, but they would definitely start with an advantage, because that is the *right* way. There is no permanent winning or losing when things move, as they should, in a circle. . . .

But the white men, who live in straight lines and squares, do not believe as I do . . . With them it is everything or nothing, Washita or Greasy Grass . . . Winning is all they care about, and if they can do that by scratching a pen across a paper or saying something into the wind, they are much happier. . . .

Old Lodge Skins was right about the army wanting to win. Crook's defeat at the Rosebud had embarrassed the army, and the debacle at the Little Bighorn shamed it. The nation, of course, was outraged. By August of 1876 Crook and Terry were lumbering around with a reassuring force of some four thousand soldiers. Naturally they found few Indians. Crazy Horse was somewhere near Bear Butte, harrying the miners in the Black Hills pretty much as the mood struck him. There was a minor engagement or two, of little note. The Indians were not suicidal — they left the massive force alone. Crook and Terry were such respecters now that they were bogged down by their own might.

In the fall of that year the whites, having failed to buy the Black Hills, simply took them. There was a travesty of a treaty council at which the theme of farming was again accented. Young Man Afraid, after hearing a great deal about farming, sarcastically ventured the view that it might take him one hundred years to learn how to do such work — he wanted to make sure that the government meant to take care of his people well during this learning period. With this disgraceful treaty the Indians lost not only the Black Hills but the Powder River, the Yellowstone, the Bighorns. There was even talk of moving the settled Sioux at the Red Cloud and Spotted Tail agencies to a reservation on the Missouri River, a move they all bitterly resisted. Crook, at this point, wanted to depose Red Cloud, insisting that he had not been forceful enough when it came to bringing in the hostiles. He wanted to promote Spotted

Tail, not because he was better about the hostiles but because he was somewhat easier to deal with than the argumentative Bad Face.

From this point in 1876 on, the bitter factionalism of agency politics — in the Sioux's case, the factionalism of the defeated — has a place in the story. Everyone was getting more than a little tired of Red Cloud, but he was both tenacious and smart. He was to be one of the very few Plains Indian leaders of this period who survived everything, dying of old age in 1909.

By the late fall of 1876 General Crook had been in the field for almost a year, with no significant victories and one embarrassing defeat, the Rosebud. In November he finally had a victory, hitting the Cheyennes under Dull Knife and Little Wolf in their winter camp in the Bighorns. The Cheyennes who got away struggled north in weather so terrible that eleven babies froze in one night; when the survivors finally reached Crazy Horse, he took them in and provided for them as best he could.

By the end of what was in some ways a year of glory, 1876, Crazy Horse had to face the fact that his people had come to a desperate pass. It was a terrible winter, with subzero temperatures day after day. The Indians were ragged and hungry; the soldiers who opposed them were warmly clothed and well equipped. The victories of the previous summer were, to the Sioux and the Cheyennes, now just memories. They had little ammunition and were hard pressed to find game enough to feed themselves.

Colonel Nelson A. Miles, then camped on the Tongue River, badly wanted Crazy Horse's surrender. (Though he couldn't have known it at the time, if he could have persuaded Crazy Horse to come in to his camp he would have ended up claiming three great surrenders, the other two being Chief Joseph and Geronimo.) To entice Crazy Horse, Miles sent many runners promising fair treatment for himself and his people.

Near the end of the year Crazy Horse apparently decided he had better consider this offer. He approached, but stopped well short of Miles's camp and sent a number of emissaries ahead to discuss the matter. Unfortunately, some of Miles's Crow scouts saw the Oglalas coming and attacked them, killing several. Miles was furious when he heard of this and tried to

143

make amends, but the damage was done. Crazy Horse turned back.

When the New Year came, Miles attacked and kept attacking until the weather finally stopped him. Crazy Horse moved north and hung on. It was during this time that he is said to have shot the horses of Sioux who wanted to give up and go to the agencies, a charge that is still debated.

During this hard period, with the soldiers just waiting for spring to begin another series of attacks, Sitting Bull decided to take himself and his people to Canada. Crazy Horse perhaps considered this option, but rejected it. It may have been because in Canada it was even colder — or it may have been because he just didn't want to leave home.

17

The winter of 1876–77 was very hard. The fact that the soldiers had been willing to fight until the middle of January was evidence of a new determination on the part of the military to finish the job and subdue the Plains Indians once and for all. Only a few of the Indian leaders still holding out were much to be feared, Crazy Horse being one of these. In general, that long, bitter winter was a time of wearing down.

Very probably, during these months, Crazy Horse finally realized that he would not be able to live out his life as a free man — a resister. During these months he wandered off alone so often that He Dog reproached him for it, reminding him that there were people who depended on him. Crazy Horse was not a chief in the sense that Old Man Afraid had been a chief, but he did have followers, several hundred cold, ill-clad people who looked to him for guidance and provision. When he tried a second time to come in, in early May of 1877, he had nine hundred people with him, and more than two thousand horses.

It was a surrender, of a sort, but only of a sort. Crook claimed it, though Crazy Horse actually first sat down with Lieutenant Philo Clark. Even so, it was not a full or normal surrender, and neither the agency Indians (whether Red Cloud's or Spotted Tail's) nor the generals nor, probably, Crazy Horse himself ever quite believed that a true surrender had taken place. They may all have intuited an essential truth, which was that Crazy Horse was not tamable, not a man of politics. He could only assist his people as warrior and hunter — a bureaucrat he was not. Had there not been those nine hundred people looking to him for help, he might have elected to do what Geronimo did for so long: take a few warriors and a few women and stay out. He might have gone deep into the hills with a few men and fought as a guerrilla until someone betrayed him or at least outshot him. But it was true that these nine hundred people depended on him, so he brought them in and sat down, for the first time, in council with the white men.

He came into Red Cloud's agency, at Fort Robinson in northwestern Nebraska. I think it is fair to say that neither Red Cloud nor Spotted Tail nor any of the leading agency Indians were happy to see him. Perhaps Crook, who soon arrived, was the one happy person. With Sitting Bull in Canada and Crazy Horse settled near an agency, Three Stars could wipe his brow in relief. Also, Crook, not Miles, got credit for the surrender, which made up a little for the embarrassment on the Rosebud.

This august event, the surrender of "Chief" Crazy Horse, was reported in *The New York Times*, May 8, 1877.

18

From the time that Crazy Horse handed over his rifle and his horses to the white officers at Fort Robinson until his death just four months later, he was a confused, stressed, off-balance, and, finally, desperate man. For almost the first time in his life he had done something he really didn't believe in, something that went directly against his nature. Even though he knew he had done it for the right reason — the welfare of the people — it did not feel right. The adjustments required of him if he was to live as an agency Indian were not adjustments he was able to make. From his personal point of view probably the best thing that came out of this move was that Dr. (later Agent) Valentine McGillycuddy offered to treat Black Shawl, his wife, for her tuberculosis, and did treat her with some success.

Before Crazy Horse surrendered, Crook made two promises that he was later unwilling or unable to keep. He wanted this surrender, and to get it he offered Crazy Horse an agency of his own, in country of his choosing; and he also promised the Sioux generally that they would be allowed to leave the agencies and go on a forty-day buffalo hunt. These promises may have been made rashly, but they were not necessarily made insincerely. A good many commanders in the field made well-reasoned promises to the Indians, only to have them rejected by someone higher up the ladder of command. Nelson A. Miles later made promises both to Chief Joseph and to Geronimo that he himself considered practical — in the case of Chief Joseph, at least, Miles was somewhat dismayed by the brusqueness with which his plans for the Nez Percé were rejected by the higher-ups. This tendency of the War Department to ignore whatever had been promised by a man in the field was particularly hard on lower-level officers and agents. They would only work effectively with the agency Indians if they held the Indians' trust, but it was impossible to hold any Indian's trust when they were continually having to explain that no, they couldn't do what they had just said they *would* do.

Crook at first probably thought it made sense to allow a buffalo hunt. It would have reduced Indian dependence on government goods somewhat, and given an active people something to do other than sit around waiting for handouts. It would also have allowed them to retain at least a few of the rhythms of their old life, which would have been a big boost to Sioux morale. But Crook soon began to have second thoughts about boosting Sioux morale all that much. It meant rearming people he had just disarmed, risking — with Crazy Horse particularly — the possibility that they would then try to reclaim another part of their old life: the part that involved fighting whites.

There was, too, another factor in the rescinding of these promises. The first thing the whites liked to do with a great hostile was to dress him up and whisk him off to Washington to meet the president and other high potentates, thus, it was hoped, impressing him with the immensity of white power. It usually worked, too. Even Sitting Bull, once he saw the east, was impressed by white power, but was correspondingly depressed by the homeless beggars he encountered on the streets of the white men's cities. Such a lack of charity would never have been allowed among the Sioux, he pointed out.

A second reason for taking major hostiles east was to neutralize them. A bit of lionizing, a little ceremony, it was felt, would make them that much less likely to take again the path of war. Instead of fighting, the hostile would soon settle down and become part of the process of democratic life.

Where Crazy Horse was concerned, this policy was an utter failure. He never became part of the process, which is surely one big reason he is such a hero today. He did, however, entertain the notion of going to Washington. The problem was that he insisted that at least one of General Crook's promises be kept *before he went:* if he could have his agency, or if there could be a hunt, *then* he would go to meet the president. If the whites had immediately given him the agency he wanted — on Beaver Creek, in the Powder River country — then he might have gone to Washington and might, just conceivably, have adjusted. But he was determined to get *something* before he made the trip; also, he was probably just nervous.

One reason he was adamant about having his own agency was that he didn't like it where he was. At Red Cloud's agency the attitude of the settled Sioux toward him was at best ambivalent and at worst malign. Red Cloud and Spotted Tail, still bitterly jealous of one another, were even more jealous of Crazy Horse, in part because he still had the aura of the warrior about him. He had, after all, been in a shooting war with Miles as recently as January. Though he had been forced to move, he had not been decisively beaten, and he had done the right thing by taking in the Cheyennes who had been dispossessed by Crook.

From the day that Crazy Horse came in he was the focus of rumor, envy, jealousy, and hatred, and it was among his own people that the hatred became a dripping, ultimately fatal poison — a paradoxical thing since, except for this short terrible period, no Indian was more respected by the Indian people than he was. Captain John Gregory Bourke, who served with Crook, said that he had never heard an Indian speak of Crazy Horse with anything but respect. And yet, during this one period, the mere fact that the white officers respected him for fighting them so hard in battle made the agency Indians jealous. What they were jealous of, finally, was his moral authority. Among a broken people an unbroken man can only rarely be tolerated — he becomes a too-painful reminder of what the people as a whole had once been.

As I read the records, Crazy Horse at this point was far from being broken, but he was certainly very stressed.

Even though he camped twice as far from Fort Robinson as he was supposed to, he was still in much closer proximity to white people than he had been since his youth on the Platte. He was worried about his people, worried about his wife, and confused by what the whites seemed to want of him. Though there were among the whites men who respected him and some who just liked him, he must often have wished that he had continued to hold out. For a time he fidgeted and worried, waiting for the whites to either give him his agency or allow his people to go on the hunt that had been promised.

The whites did neither. Crook pestered Crazy Horse to go to Washington, but Crazy Horse kept backing out. The summer was usually a time of pleasure for the Sioux, but this summer — 1877 — was for Crazy Horse a time of confusion and anxiety.

Meanwhile, the poisons of idleness and jealousy were working on the Sioux. An Indian named Grabber began to spread the rumor that the whites liked Crazy Horse so much that they were going to make him chief of all the Sioux, though at this time he wasn't really chief of any of the Sioux. Jealousy intensified as rumors of his ascendancy multiplied. The whites were as uncertain about him as the Sioux, although one or two experienced officers recognized that he was just off-balance, overwhelmed by his new situation. Too many whites had talked to him too much — and this was an Indian who had never parleyed with white men before. He didn't know how to assess the conflicting statements he heard them make.

A few wise officers advised that he be left alone until he calmed down a little and had time to adjust to agency life, but this advice was ignored. Crazy Horse was the star of the hour — everyone wanted to talk to him. Probably he would have weakened and eventually gone to Washington — after all, he had little to do — but Red Cloud didn't like it that this upstart was suddenly such a big star. Neither he nor Spotted Tail wanted Crazy Horse to be taken east and lionized: they began to talk against him.

One legitimate apprehension the Indian leaders may have had about Crazy Horse was the fear that if he misbehaved, the government might react by immediately dragging them off to the Missouri River reservation. By this time most of the Sioux leaders feared that the Missouri would be their eventual fate (and it was).

Though many of the whites who met Crazy Horse liked him, the agency Indians continued to talk against him. Crook was annoyed by Crazy Horse's reluctance to go to Washington. Some time around midsummer of 1877 the higher thinking came to be that perhaps the best thing to do with this Indian was to send him to prison in Florida, before he broke out and became a rallying point for the discontented young warriors, most of whom, having no chance to either fight or hunt, were bored silly.

Then, to everyone's surprise, in far-off Idaho, the Nez Percé broke out first and began their dramatic thirteen-hundred-mile march through Idaho, Wyoming, and Montana, whipping up on everybody they encountered along the way. At first no one supposed Looking Glass and Chief Joseph would get very far, or cause as much alarm as they caused; but the next thing anybody knew they had whipped yet more militia and were speeding along a clear track to Canada. One-armed General Howard was chasing them, but he wasn't catching them — Crook eventually became responsible for trying to head them off. Lieutenant

Philo Clark, the officer who did most of the dealing with Crazy Horse, seems to have gotten it into his head that the idle Oglalas could be useful in this effort. Crook seems to have briefly entertained this notion — his options at the time were not good. The meeting that was held to discuss this matter can only have added to Crazy Horse's confusion. He had come in, given up his gun, and promised to fight no more, but now the whites wanted to give him his gun again and have him fight the Nez Percé. Where was the sense in all of it? Indeed, there was no sense. The army had a superabundance of Sioux at its disposal, not to mention plenty of Crows and Shoshones. Why arm the one Sioux leader who was most likely to stay out once he got out? The Oglalas didn't seem the most logical choices anyway — their range was well east of the Nez Percé's looping line of flight.

Crazy Horse was again reluctant; he may have supposed that this was some complicated plot on Crook's part to get him to help fight Sitting Bull. Or he may simply have had no idea what was going on with these whites. Though the whites and the Indians lived in close proximity at the agencies, neither group had any clear notion of what the other group was thinking or saying or planning.

Also, Crazy Horse may simply have been irritated by this white effort to get him to fight the Nez Percé. His attitude may have been: Why me? Parleys annoyed him, tried his patience, disturbed him. Crook wasn't at this one, anyway. Crazy Horse finally told the whites that he had promised to be a man of peace, but if the whites insisted that he go fight the Nez Percé he would fight them until every last Nez Percé was killed — the kind of claim that probably just reflected his exasperation.

At this point a famous mistranslation occurred, made by Crazy Horse's old friend Frank Grouard, the scout. Grouard reportedly told the whites that Crazy Horse meant to fight until every last *white man* was killed. The half-breed scout Billy Garnett, who had known Crazy Horse most of his life, was aghast and — along with others who understood Sioux — immediately tried to correct Grouard, but whether they convinced anyone is now hard to say. Mari Sandoz makes much of this mistranslation; George Hyde makes little. My own feeling is that the incident speaks mainly to the intense climate of suspicion that surrounded everything Crazy Horse did in the last few days of his life. Frank Grouard was a mixed-blood who had interpreted at many councils; Crazy Horse liked him. That Grouard lied in such a way as to get Crazy Horse in more trouble than he was in already is explainable mainly by jealousy, if it is explainable at all. Or it may be that Grouard himself wanted to twit the whites, even shock them; it could even be that he was drunk and misunderstood, or that Crazy Horse was so bored with the whole proceeding that he made an outrageous remark merely to end the meeting.

All we know now is that this incident did nothing to lessen or allay white paranoia where Crazy Horse was concerned. He was clearly unhappy at the agency, clearly missed the freedom of the plains. Of all the Indians at Red Cloud's agency he *was* the one most likely to fight again; only an exceptionally obtuse officer could have missed that fact.

On the other hand, immense grief always flowed from the army's tendency to see war where there was no war. They had a hard time understanding that the Indians they had subdued would really stay subdued. The slightest sign of Indian independence invariably produced an overreaction on the part of the white authorities, the best example of which is white response to the Ghost Dance.

It is hard now to understand, except as paranoia, the overreaction to the Ghost Dance, or other, earlier expressions of Indian messianic or millennial religion. The Paiute holy man Wovoka, who lived in Nevada and began to preach the Ghost Dance in the summer of 1887, had been anticipated nearly a decade earlier by the Apache preacher Noch-ay-del-kline, who lived on Cibecue Creek in Arizona. The army was so alarmed by Noch-ay-del-kline's preaching and the response it evoked in the local Apaches that they went to arrest him, although he was at the time living peaceably at home. Eighteen men were killed in this arrest. Geronimo, who had been trying to live as the whites wanted him to, read this lesson well and soon went out again, into the mountains of Mexico.

The white authorities hugely overreacted to both these native preachers, who offered to raise the good spirits of the dead while burying the bad people under a new soil. What they preached, that is — allowing for all differences — was not so very different from what low-Protestant, millennial, evangelical, Holy Roller charismatics preach now to dirt-poor congregations throughout rural America. To broken, despairing, poverty-stricken people the Apocalypse has always sounded good. Sitting Bull was killed because he wouldn't try to suppress the Ghost Dance on his reservation. It is unlikely that he himself believed Wovoka, or that Geronimo believed Noch-ay-del-kline — both men were too hardheaded — but they both recognized that the preachers brought a beaten and depressed people a little involvement and a little hope. The whites saw this merely as a sign that the Indians might act up again, so eighteen died at Cibecue Creek and as many as two hundred at Wounded Knee.

19

The incident that speaks most decisively to the climate of suspicion surrounding Crazy Horse occurred at the beginning of September 1877, when General Crook was coming to Fort Robinson to a council about the Nez Percé problem. On the way to the council Crook was met by an Indian named Woman's Dress, who warned him that Crazy Horse meant to shake his hand and then stab him to death. Crook may possibly have known about the famous mistranslation by then, in which Crazy Horse had reportedly said that he would kill all the whites to the last man; but George Crook was not a man who liked to turn aside. Once he started for a place — as he often said — he liked to get there. Crook surely know enough by then to disregard most Indian gossip. Had there not been such a climate of suspicion surrounding Crazy Horse, it is not likely he would have paid Woman's Dress much mind. For all Crook knew, Crazy Horse didn't even plan to show up at the council, and very likely Crazy

Horse wouldn't have. But Crook took this wild threat seriously and for once made an excuse and turned aside.

Shortly after this, Crook ordered Crazy Horse's arrest, a move he surely knew would be touchy. Crazy Horse, after all, had come in as a great military hero; he had beaten Crook himself, helped destroy Custer, checked Miles. He was a hero to the young men — the first generation of young Sioux men, it should be remembered, who were not allowed to establish their bravery as warriors in the normal way. These young men were looking for a leader, and Crazy Horse was the natural — in fact, the only — choice.

Crook, though, had no real grounds for arresting Crazy Horse, who had been behaving correctly. But Red Cloud and Spotted Tail were wild to be rid of him, and he made the white military men nervous. Crook had plans to send him to Florida — some say to Fort Jefferson in the Dry Tortugas, the prison-atoll for incorrigibles. (Even Geronimo, who, for a period, killed every white he ran into, only got sent to Fort Marion, a palace by comparison.)

Early in September, though, a huge force of soldiers and Indian policemen went to Crazy Horse's camp to arrest him, only to find that he had just left for the Spotted Tail agency, forty miles away. The pursuers followed him all day but could not catch up; the scout Billy Garnett says this was because Crazy Horse had a method for keeping his horses fresh: he walked them going uphill, loped them when he was going down. No Water, still jealous because Crazy Horse had briefly made off with Black Buffalo Woman, is said to have ruined two horses in this pursuit (and then billed the government for them), but the arresting force never quite caught up.

When Crazy Horse arrived, his uncle Spotted Tail was anything but happy to see him. He told Crazy Horse unequivocally that he was the boss at his agency: if Crazy Horse expected to stay, he would have to toe the line and obey all orders. Spotted Tail wanted no trouble and Crazy Horse was a magnet for it — a magnet so powerful that as many as a thousand Indians may have joined or at least watched the arresting party.

Crazy Horse considered that he *had* been behaving well; he was at a loss to understand why so many of his own people would show up to help arrest him. Agent Jesse Lee, whom he liked and trusted, came to speak to him. Crazy Horse explained, again, that he *had* offered to fight the Nez Percé, that he *hadn't* said anything about killing the whites to the last man, that he had never had the slightest intention of stabbing Crook in a council, etc. So why was there all this fuss?

Agent Lee, who got on well with Crazy Horse, accepted his explanations. But he said that, nonetheless, it would be necessary for Crazy Horse to come back to Fort Robinson and explain all this to General Bradley, the fort's commander.

The next day, September 6, 1877, Crazy Horse went back, followed, if not surrounded, by a huge mass of warriors and soldiers. He was by then desperate — and justly so. Why did so many Indians — among them several of his oldest allies — so obviously hate him and want his blood? He was now not the hunter; he was the hunted. This man who had once had the whole of the Great Plains as his home suddenly had no place to be.

No one really knows how many Indians rode with him from the Spotted Tail agency that day, or how many were waiting at Fort Robinson when, near dusk, he rode in. There were so many that the mere mass must have stressed him more. He was a man who had always liked to be alone, and now, suddenly, most of the nation he had been born into was massed around him. No doubt he would far rather have been living in a cave or a hole — but for that it was too late.

As Crazy Horse understood matters, he had made no threat and committed no offense. How could he have understood that he had become an intolerable symbol of resistance, even though he wasn't resisting? But he was, for white and Indian alike, a symbol of resistance so potent that neither could afford to leave him alive and free.

On the ride back to Fort Robinson, according to Agent Jesse Lee, Crazy Horse was hopeful one moment and desperately worried the next, a natural alternation of mood under the circumstances. Spotted Tail and Touch-the-Clouds rode back with him, along with many of Spotted Tail's warriors. Perhaps Crazy Horse knew, as Malcolm X did toward the end, that very soon his own people were going to have his blood.

Near dusk the great party came into the valley of the White River and rode onto the parade ground of the fort. Many Indians were waiting, but a path opened for Crazy Horse. He had time to say a few words to his old friend He Dog before walking with

Agent Lee to what he supposed would be his promised interview with General Bradley.

As he approached the official quarters his old friend Little Big Man, now an ambitious Indian policeman, stepped close beside him, ready to fulfill, possibly for the second time, the old prophecy Crazy Horse had dreamed as a boy. What Crazy Horse thought about Little Big Man's metamorphosis into Indian policeman we don't know, but Little Big Man was hardly the only one of his former allies to take that route to preferment. Young Man Afraid was an Indian policeman, and no one thought the worse of him for it.

General Bradley had no intention of seeing Crazy Horse and no interest in hearing his side of the story, a painful discovery not only for Crazy Horse but for Agent Lee also. Bradley's orders were clear: Crazy Horse was to be arrested and shipped immediately to Omaha and thence to Florida. Agent Lee, whether knowingly or unknowingly, had made a major false promise, one that was to haunt him for years. (For some weeks after that night he expected to be killed by Crazy Horse partisans.)

Crazy Horse surely thought he was going

to see the camp commander when Little Big Man and Lieutenant Kenningston (the officer of the day) led him past the adjutant's office toward the guardhouse. But the moment he saw, or smelled, the filthy cells where the chained Indians were kept, he sensed betrayal and whirled, attempting to run back into the parade ground. He was scarcely clear of the doorway when Little Big Man jumped on his back and tried to hold his arms. Little Big Man was stout — Crazy Horse could not immediately shake him, but they were not struggling alone anymore; they were in full view of the many, many Indians on the parade ground, most but not all of whom were, at this moment, hostile to Crazy Horse. He had managed to conceal a knife under his blanket and he finally got one arm free and cut Little Big Man, causing him to loosen his hold.

When it looked for a brief few seconds as if Crazy Horse might break free and make a fight of it, even though he had only a knife (some say he had two knives; Billy Garnett thought he even had a pistol), there was a short, bitter spew of epithets from those Sioux who wanted him dead: "Shoot him!" "Stab him!" "Shoot the son-of-a-bitch!" Frank Grouard remembered a moment of silence, and then the sound of hammers being cocked and shells being chambered in many rifles. Billy Garnett thought some of the chained prisoners ran out; he remembered the clanking of chains. Some say that several rifles were raised but that the officer of the day knocked them down. A white private, William Gentles, who was to die of asthma about six months later, ran forward and bayoneted Crazy Horse twice (some say only once; Little Big Man says not at all) as he struggled to free himself. One of Private Gentles's thrusts missed — the bayonet stuck in the wood of the doorjamb. There is disagreement about the bayoneting, but what is certain is that one thrust pierced the kidneys, causing Crazy Horse to sink down, a mortally wounded man.

20

Our century has seen several public assassinations to which there were many eyewitnesses, as many in some cases as there were in Fort Robinson, Nebraska, that September night. We've had JFK, his brother Robert, Martin Luther King, Malcolm X, to name a few. Invariably the men and women who were there each had their own memories of these killings, and the memories differ greatly in matters of detail.

So it was with the death of Crazy Horse; many saw him killed and their memories differ. With the exception of Little Big Man, who maintained to the end that Crazy Horse, in his whirling frenzy, accidentally and fatally stabbed himself, all the witnesses agree that Little Big Man tried to hold him, that many were ready to shoot him, that other Indians grabbed him, that Private Gentles stabbed him (and also the doorjamb). There is a pictographic record of the stabbing, done by Amos Bad Heart Bull. Crazy Horse's arms were held by his own people, just as the dream said they would be. Crazy Horse sank down, his blood seeping into the dust of the parade ground. Those loyal to him and those ready to kill him faced off for a few moments of almost unbearably high tension. All agree that had a single shot been fired there would have been a terrible carnage, with Indians fighting Indians and Indians fighting soldiers, without anyone quite knowing why they were shooting or even whom they were shooting at, there in the gathering dusk on the parade ground of a small fort in the west.

The high, keening tension held only until it began to be realized that Crazy Horse had been dealt a fatal blow.

Then the tension broke. No shot was fired, and Crazy Horse — a man who had lost his brother, his daughter, the woman he loved, several friends, his way of life, and even, for a time, his people — began his leaving as a man and his arrival as a myth, a man around whom stories that are like little gospels accumulate. A variorum death of Crazy Horse would consist of at least a score of versions, all contributed or recollected by people, white and red, who were in the fort that night.

These recollections, of course, diverge on many points of detail, overlap, contradict one another; probably most of them are partly true, probably none of them can be said to be completely, definitively true. Violence produces shock, and shock distorts memory: a patrolman trying to sort out varying versions of a rush-hour car wreck has the same problem as the biographer of Crazy Horse. Many saw what happened, but no two witnesses remembered it exactly the same.

Not long before Crazy Horse left for the Spotted Tail agency he had a much-reported conversation with his old friend He Dog. Crook wanted all the Sioux at Red Cloud to move across the creek, nearer to White Butte, so he would have them handy for a big council. Crazy Horse didn't want to move across the creek, but He Dog thought it might be best to do as he was told. He was nervous, though, about what this move might mean for their friendship, so he asked Crazy Horse if such a move on his part would mean that they were enemies now. Crazy Horse laughed, perhaps for the last time; then he reminded He Dog that he was not speaking to a white man. Whites were the only ones, he said, who made rules for other people. Camp where you please.

So it is with the death of Crazy Horse:

the reader is invited to camp where he or she pleases amid the many recollections and recountings.

Crazy Horse, right after receiving the fatal wound, cried out, "Let me go, my friend — you have hurt me plenty bad!" or words to that effect. Then he sank down. Once the high tension between the two groups died, two or three people claim to have stepped forward and covered Crazy Horse with a blanket. He Dog says he tore Crazy Horse's own blanket in two and covered him with half of it, which seems odd. Why not cover him with all of it? Then Dr. McGillycuddy came, looked at the wounds, saw how it was. Some say that Little Big Man howled when Crazy Horse whirled and cut him; others say Crazy Horse merely cut him on the thumb. Lieutenant Clark was sound asleep, perhaps drunk — his men had to sling him around roughly to get him awake. The dying man on the parade ground was still under arrest; the orders were to put him in the guardhouse. General Bradley would not, at first, relax the order. But when the soldiers started to move the wounded Crazy Horse to the guardhouse, Touch-the-Clouds intervened. Touch-the-Clouds said that Crazy Horse was a chief. He could not be put in the guardhouse.

The Indians, now, were quiet — perhaps chastened, perhaps numbed. Many among them, some of them his old allies, realized that for reasons of politics they had killed a man who had no politics, just the conviction that he wanted to live his life in accordance with the precepts of his own people, as he had been taught to live it.

There were a lot of Indians on the parade ground, and they were mainly, now, on the side of Touch-the-Clouds. Dr. McGillycuddy had to go twice to General Bradley to persuade him not to attempt to move this dying Indian to the guardhouse. The general was irritated by all this; perhaps he thought Crazy Horse was shamming. Not until Dr. McGillycuddy convinced him there would be a very big fight if such a move was attempted did the general relent and allow Crazy Horse to be taken into the adjutant's office instead.

This move the Sioux allowed, although they would rather have moved him outside the fort and let him die with the rites of Sioux tradition, as Conquering Bear had died so long before. Once in the office Crazy Horse refused a cot and was put on the floor. Exactly who was with him in his last hours is unclear. Mari Sandoz says both his parents were allowed in; others mention only his father, Worm. Touch-the-Clouds, after surrendering his weapons, was allowed to go in. Ian Frazier thinks that the fact that Crazy Horse refused the cot and died on the floor meant that he was his own man to the end.

In Peter Nabokov's *Native American Testimony* there is a Crazy Horse deathbed statement — Evan Connell Jr. thinks this statement was taken down by Baptiste Pourier, the fort's interpreter. But neither Mari Sandoz nor He Dog nor most other accounts of his death mention Baptiste Pourier. Here, for what it is worth, is the statement, supposedly spoken to Agent Jesse Lee:

My friend, I do not blame you for this. Had I listened to you this trouble would not have happened to me. I was not hostile to the white man. Sometimes my young men would attack the Indians who were their enemies and took their ponies. They did it in return.

We had buffalo for food, and their hides for clothing, and our tipis. We preferred hunting to a life of idleness on the reservations, where we were driven against our will. At times we did not get enough to eat, and we were not allowed to leave the reservation to hunt.

We preferred our own way of living. We were no expense to the government then. All we wanted was peace and to be left alone. Soldiers were sent out in the winter, who destroyed our villages. Then "Long Hair" came in the same way. They say we massacred him but he would have done the same to us had we not defended ourselves and fought to the last. Our first impulse was to escape with our squaws and papooses, but we were so hemmed in we had to fight.

After that I went up on Tongue River with a few of my people and lived in peace. But the government would not let me alone. Finally, I came back to the Red Cloud agency . . . I came here with the agent to talk to the Big White Chief, but was not given a chance. They tried to confine me, I tried to escape, and a soldier ran his bayonet into me.

I have spoken.

In contrast to this lengthy speech, Black Elk maintained that Crazy Horse said only three words after he was stabbed: "Hey, hey, hey!" an expression of regret. Though

Crazy Horse may indeed have wanted to assure Agent Lee that he didn't blame him for what had happened, such a long apologia seems peculiar for a man who had never liked to talk and who, moreover, would have had little interest in neatly tidying up the record.

Others say that his father, Worm, spoke to him at some point, saying, "Son, I am here." Crazy Horse then roused himself long enough to say, "Father, it is no good for the people to depend on me any longer — I am bad hurt." In its tragic simplicity this exchange between father and son puts us back with the Greeks.

Some say that soldiers came and went — others say that only Dr. McGillycuddy came and went.

If the last exchange between father and son — assuming we have it more or less correct — is like the Greeks, Touch-the-Clouds' final tribute is quietly Shakespearean. When he saw that Crazy Horse was dead, he pulled the blanket over him and said: "This is the lodge of Crazy Horse." He may also have said: "This is good. He sought death and now he has found it."

If it is true that the destination the government had in mind for him was a cell dug into the coral on the Dry Tortugas, then Touch-the-Clouds was right. A man who had lived his whole life under the great western skies would not have lasted long in any prison. Sitting Bull, Spotted Tail, and Geronimo all survived the white man's prison, but the Kiowa chief Satanta did not. He found confinement so irksome that he jumped head first from a high window. Crazy Horse, daring and brave as a warrior, was in other ways not as tough a nut as Sitting Bull or Geronimo. It is hard to imagine him signing photographs for tourists at the big St. Louis Exposition, as Geronimo did — always insisting on his price, one dollar.

But that is speculation. The fact is that Crazy Horse died later that night, September 6, 1877, on the floor of the adjutant's office in Fort Robinson, Nebraska.

When Touch-the-Clouds went out to bring the news of his death to the waiting Sioux, a wail and a howling went up from the parade ground and from the many, many tents, near and distant: a wailing and a howling of grief, of fear, of torment, frustration, despair. No Sioux had exceeded him in charity. The women remembered the charity — it was the women who wailed and howled in the night.

Someone mentioned that taps was played, which seems extremely unlikely. The wailing of the women of the Brulé and Oglala Sioux was the taps for Crazy Horse.

Many of the white people in the fort that night expected to be killed. The fact that the Sioux themselves had meant to kill Crazy Horse — and had helped — meant nothing now. Agent Jesse Lee was sure he faced certain death for having led Crazy Horse back to Fort Robinson; he even instructed his wife in how to kill herself, should they be overwhelmed.

The Sioux, however, did not revolt. They had plenty of leaders, but the one who had never learned to walk the white man's road was dead on the floor.

Mrs. Jesse Lee, the agent's wife, said it made her blood boil to think of all the promises made to the Indians and then broken. Angie Johnson, the captain's wife, seconded that sentiment. Whatever their views on Indians generally, these women didn't like broken promises. Both wrote in outrage to their families.

The same two women, and several men as well, testified to the terrible, pitiable, Lear-like grief of Crazy Horse's parents: they wandered the fort for three days, sobbing, wailing, rending their garments, refusing all succor. When they were finally allowed to have their son's body, they put it on a burial scaffold outside the fort. Later, when the miserable, predictable exodus to the Missouri River began, they took his body on a travois and then slipped off and buried him. Nobody knows exactly where he is buried, but legend has it that his burial spot is close to the creek called Wounded Knee. It is of course near this same creek that the Ghost Dance Massacre occurred, on the last day of 1890.

General Miles, perhaps vexed that he had failed to get his surrender, called Crazy Horse "the embodiment of ferocity."

General Crook, though, seems always to have regretted that he had let Woman's Dress turn him away from that last council. He had, no doubt, by then figured out that Woman's Dress was a shit-stirrer, a "two-edged sword to his own people," as one Sioux described him.

An old Sioux who wouldn't give his name to Mari Sandoz or Elinor Hinman said: "I'm not telling anyone — white or Indian — what I know about the killing of Crazy Horse. That affair was a disgrace and a dirty shame. We killed our own man."

Before Crazy Horse was even in the

ground, Little Big Man and a delegation of the Sioux leaders were in Washington to discuss the relocation issue. There exists a curious artifact, a medal presumably given Little Big Man for his bravery in subduing Crazy Horse. Who made this medal, and who issued it, are not clear. President Hayes may have had a few medals struck off, but none are known to exist for the other members of the delegation. This medal is on loan to the Nebraska State Historical Association.

It may be true, as Black Elk says, that Crazy Horse during his life never owned a very good horse; but he has a powerful horse now: a horse as strong as a mountain. If the Ziolkowski family can only keep it up, he will finally — in a few more years, and in spirit at least — have risen forever over the Black Hills. He will have managed to take back the road General Custer opened: the road the Sioux call the Thieves' Road.

Sources

Ambrose, Stephen E. *Crazy Horse and Custer: The Parallel Lives of Two American Warriors.* New York: Doubleday, 1975.
A good book, though not free of abundant speculation. The author is riding a hobbyhorse and keeps it in a high trot throughout.

Berger, Thomas. *Little Big Man.* New York: Dial, 1964.
Easily the best novel about the Plains Indian wars. The author finesses the question of Crazy Horse thusly:

> I seen that great warrior once before we split off by ourselves: he had a face full of sharpened edges, wore no ornamentation whatever, no paint, no feathers; he was like a living weapon. He surrendered to the military a year later and was stabbed to death in a scuffle at the agency while his arms were being held by another Indian called Little Big Man — Not me. He was a Sioux and there-

fore it was a different name, though Englishing the same. . . .

Bourke, John Gregory. *On the Border with Crook*. New York: Scribner's, 1881.
A famous memoir, much reprinted, and still readable. The author went on to write a famous work of anthropology, *Scatological Rites of All Nations* (1891).

Brininstool, E. A. *Crazy Horse, the Invincible Oglala Sioux Chief*. Los Angeles, 1949.

Brown, Dee. *Bury My Heart at Wounded Knee: An Indian History of the American West*. New York: Holt, 1971.
Not an Indian History history but a valuable overall account nonetheless.

Clark, Robert A. *The Killing of Chief Crazy Horse*. Glendale: Arthur H. Clark, 1976.
Contains the scout Billy Garnett's account, which differs in some respects from all the others.

Connell, Evan S. Jr. *Son of the Morning Star*. San Francisco: North Point, 1984.
Its topic may be Custer and the Little Bighorn, but its theme is the American character, as revealed in the struggle for

the Great Plains.

DeMaillie, Raymond (ed.). *The Sixth Grandfather.* Lincoln: University of Nebraska, 1984.
In 1932 the writer John G. Neihardt published *Black Elk Speaks*, his attempt to preserve the teachings of the Sioux holy man Black Elk, whose father had been a contemporary of Crazy Horse. There has long been debate about how much of the book is Black Elk and how much is Neihardt. *The Sixth Grandfather* contains a kind of digest of the memories and teachings of Black Elk, as given in the interviews recorded by Neihardt's daughters, Hilda and Enid. These are the rough interviews, stripped of the literary art with which Neihardt later rendered them.

Frazier, Ian. *Great Plains.* New York: Farrar, Straus & Giroux, 1989.
Chapter 6, pp. 93–119, is a fine meditation on Crazy Horse.

Heyen, William. *Crazy Horse in Stillness.* Brockport, N.Y.: Boa Editions, 1996.
A powerful book of poetry, showing that the imagining and reimagining still goes on.

Hyde, George E. *Red Cloud's Folk*. Norman: University of Oklahoma, 1937; and *Spotted Tail's Folk*. Norman: University of Oklahoma, 1961.

George E. Hyde deserves a short biography himself. Rendered completely deaf and nearly blind while in his early twenties, he had to do his scholarly work entirely through correspondence, and with the resources of the Omaha Public Library, or what it could obtain for him. Despite these handicaps, his histories respectively of the Oglala and the Brulé Sioux have not been bettered. They are very lively reads. He didn't think Sioux memory was any worse than white memory, but he didn't think it was any better, either. He was cranky and impatient, but a very good analyst of the often inconsistent and contradictory sources.

Kadlecek, Edward, and Mabell Kadlecek. *To Kill an Eagle: Indian Views on the Death of Crazy Horse*. Boulder: Johnson Books, 1981.

Gathers some interesting accounts; the more one reads about this death, the more one is likely to sink into confusion.

Manning, Richard. *Grassland.* New York: Viking, 1995.

An essential book for students of the plains.

Nabokov, Peter. *Native American Testimony.* New York: Viking, 1991.

Contains the speech Crazy Horse is said to have made on his deathbed; no source is given for it.

Sandoz, Mari. *Crazy Horse: The Strange Man of the Oglalas.* New York, 1942.

Mari Sandoz's book is still the only full-length life of Crazy Horse. Its inception was a series of interviews she and the journalist Elinor Hinman conducted with Sioux elders in 1930–31. Hinman had intended to write the biography herself but withdrew and gave her research to Mari Sandoz, who made the decision — unfortunate, I think — to tell the story from a Sioux point of view. This makes for so many narrative awkwardnesses that the book reads like an historical novel with a biographical basis. Sandoz is not nearly so critical as George Hyde was when it came to evaluating sources, whether white or Sioux. (She once "authenticated" a so-called scalp-shirt said to have belonged to Crazy Horse. This shirt, in the collection of the Nebraska State Historical Association, contains something like 491 locks of hair, but turned out to have been machine-sewn and is no longer thought to have any connection with Crazy Horse.) Nonetheless, Mari Sandoz's book has its value; it is a considered and sympathetic study of Crazy Horse the man, and of the Sioux way of life as well.

Utley, Robert. *The Indian Frontier of the American West*, 1846–1890. Albuquerque: University of New Mexico, 1984; and *The Lance and the Shield: The Life and Times of Sitting Bull*. New York: Holt, 1993.
Both are useful books.

Vestal, Stanley. *New Sources of Indian History, 1850–1891*. Norman: University of Oklahoma, 1934.
Stanley Vestal (Walter Stanley Campbell) is almost as cranky as George Hyde, with whom he frequently disagreed. This book reprints a lot of Ghost Dance material but also contains documents of wider relevance to Sioux history.

The Nebraska State Historical Association kindly made available to me a copy of the Hinman-Sandoz interviews with He Dog and others. A pamphlet reprint of these interviews is currently out of print. One can hope that someday Judge Eli Ricker's interviews, done in 1906–07, can also be reprinted — or, rather, printed. They can only be read now on microfilm.

Beyond the sources, there are stories — always the stories.

One that I like comes to us from Red Feather, the younger brother of Black Shawl, Crazy Horse's first wife.

Red Feather says that an eagle came down and walked on Crazy Horse's coffin, once he was on a scaffold outside Fort Robinson. Red Feather mentions that he had never seen an eagle do such a thing before.

A possibility that Red Feather doesn't consider is that the eagle may have stopped in hopes of making a meal and, like Mr. Hardy's little dog, was unaware that the man he was hoping to eat was Ta-Shunka-Witco, or Crazy Horse, a man of charity and a living weapon, who, in his way and in his day, had been a kind of eagle too.

The employees of Thorndike Press hope you have enjoyed this Large Print book. All our Large Print titles are designed for easy reading, and all our books are made to last. Other Thorndike Press Large Print books are available at your library, through selected bookstores, or directly from us.

For information about titles, please call:

(800) 257-5157

To share your comments, please write:

Publisher
Thorndike Press
P.O. Box 159
Thorndike, Maine 04986